Champion Your Thoughts

&

Master Your Emotions

Living *as Your* Highest Self

Harrison S. Mungal, Ph.D, PsyD

Champion Your Thoughts and Master Your Emotions

Copyright © 2025 Harrison S. Mungal

Unless otherwise identified, Scripture quotations are from

New King James Version of the Bible.

Contact author
www.agetoage.ca
www.harrisonmungal.com
Facebook: Harrison Mungal
Twitter: HarrisonandKathleen @HKrelationships
AgetoAge @agetoagec
LinkedIn: Harrison Mungal, Ph.D., PsyD
YouTube: Harrison Mungal
Phone: 905-533-1334

ABOUT *the* **AUTHOR**

Harrison Mungal, PhD, PsyD

Dr. Mungal has two doctoral degrees, one in Clinical Psychology and the other in Philosophy in Social Work, dual master's degrees in Social Work and Christian Counselling, and a Bachelor degree in Theology. He worked over 20 years in the fields of mental health and psychiatry then went into psychology. He worked with people from a wide range of backgrounds, including brain injury survivors, refugees, victims of war, PTSD victims, those struggling with mental health and in crisis. He liaison with police, hospitals, community agencies, and inpatient mental health settings.

Dr. Mungal is completely dedicated to improving the lives of his clients. He is known all over the world in over 47 nations for his deep knowledge of neuroscience, mental health, biblical studies and topics supporting individuals, couples and families and businesses.

Dr. Mungal is a highly sought-after workshop presenter who uses his practical approach to help understand the functionality of psychology and spirituality. His global impact is clear from the way he uses humour and enthusiasm to make complicated talks about mental health, addiction, relationships, and parenting at conferences, seminars, and media platforms.

Dr. Mungal's new and scientifically sound methods have been praised by many institutions, earning him awards and recogniztions. He spreads his influence by training and advising a wide range of community partners, such as respected professionals in the fields of medicine, social work, first responders, law enforcement, and senior management teams.

Dr. Mungal is a leader in cutting-edge cognitive research that looks at mental health issues like addiction, psychosis, anxiety, and depression. His work includes research on music therapy and schizophrenia, substance abuse and addictions in the food service industry, and vaccination for children under six years old.

Dr. Mungal practical therapeutic toolbox includes evidence-based therapies including Cognitive Behavioural Therapy (CBT), Cognitive Processing Therapy (CPT), Dialectical Behavioural Therapy (DBT), Thought Developmental Practice (TDP), Acceptance and Commitment Therapy (ACT). Interpersonal therapy (IPT), Motivational Interviewing Techniques, Grounding Techniques, Integrative Eclectic Therapy, Humanistic Experiential Therapy, Interpersonal Therapy, Supportive Therapy, Exposure Therapy, Visual Therapy, Psychodynamic Therapy.

Table of Contents

INTRODUCTION

I remember the exact moment I realized my thoughts were not just passing clouds—they were the architects of my entire life.

I was forty-nine years old, sitting in the parking lot of a hospital at 5:17 p.m., rain hammering the windshield while my wife sat fitfully in the passenger seat with a downcast demeanor. Our second daughter had miscarried at five months pregnant. It felt like only weeks ago that she and her husband had come to visit me at work, in the mental health intensive care unit, to bring me the good news that she was pregnant. They had given me a little undershirt that said, "I love Grandpa." I was a therapist—supposed to have answers, supposed to be the calm one, the faith-filled one. But inside my head, a riot was raging:

"This is your fault, you did not pray enough."

"You prayed wrong."

"You're a terrible father, you should have prayed when they told you the news."

"God is punishing you, like He did taking Tiho away."

"If you were a real man of God this wouldn't be happening."

The thoughts came so fast I couldn't breathe. My chest tightened, my hands shook, and for the first time in my life I understood what people meant when they said they were having a panic attack. I was drowning in my own mind, and no amount of Scripture memory or spiritual authority could pull me out.

That day in the hospital parking lot became my breaking point—and my beginning.

Because in the suffocating darkness, a single verse I had memorized as a child floated to the surface like a lifeline:

"We demolish arguments and every pretension that sets itself up against the knowledge of God, and we take captive every thought to make it obedient to Christ." (2 Corinthians 10:5)

Take captive every thought. Not some thoughts. Not the convenient ones. Every. Single. One.

I had preached that verse dozens of times, but I had never lived it. That night I whispered through tears, *"Lord, I don't know how to do this, but I'm willing. Teach me to champion my thoughts instead of letting them champion me."*

This book, *Champion Your Thoughts and Master Your Emotions*, was born in that parking lot. It is the roadmap I wish someone had handed me when my mind felt like a prison. It is the practical, Scripture-saturated, battle-tested path I have walked—often stumbling—over the past nine years to go from mental chaos to peace that genuinely surpasses understanding.

You're holding this book because somewhere inside you know there is more. More peace. More joy. More clarity. More authority over the inner world that dictates your outer reality. You are tired of mood

8 | P a g e

swings hijacking your relationships, tired of anxiety stealing your sleep, tired of toxic thought loops replaying your worst moments on an endless reel. You are tired of feeling like a victim to your own mind.

Good. Tired is holy ground. Tired is where surrender begins. Tired is where champions are forged.

As you turn these pages, you are going to discover that your mind is not a suggestion box—it is a battlefield, and the stakes are your destiny. The enemy knows that if he can control your thoughts, he can control your life. But God has given you divine weapons (Ephesians 6:12–18), and this book is about putting those weapons in your hands and teaching you how to use them with precision.

Let me show you what's waiting for you in each chapter, not as a table of contents, but as a promise of transformation.

We begin with Champion Your Thoughts, the foundational conviction that your mind belongs to Jesus and was never meant to be a dumping ground for fear, shame, and lies. You will learn that renewing your mind (Romans 12:2) is not a suggestion—it is the daily act of worship that determines whether you live as a conqueror or a captive. By the end of this chapter you will have practical tools to identify which thoughts are from God, which are from the enemy, and which are just leftover garbage from your past—and you will know exactly what to do with each one.

From there we move into Challenge Your Thoughts, because awareness without confrontation changes nothing. Most Christians know their thinking is off, but they've never been taught how to interrogate a thought the way a lawyer cross-examines a lying witness. Using the Apostle Paul's filter in Philippians 4:8, you will learn to ask ruthless questions of every thought that tries to set up camp in your mind: Is it true? Is it noble? Is it right? Is it pure? Is it lovely? Is it admirable? You will walk away from this chapter with a courtroom in your head where lies no longer get to testify unchallenged.

Then we cross the bridge to Master Your Emotions, because thoughts and feelings are married, and whichever one you feed will lead the relationship. You will discover that emotions are incredible servants but terrible masters, and that Jesus never once shamed anyone for feeling—he simply taught them how to feel without sinning (Ephesians 4:26). You will learn that emotional mastery is not the absence of emotion but the presence of Jesus in the middle of it.

Regulate Your Emotions and Triggered Emotions are companion chapters that will probably save your relationships. You will learn the physiological truth that you cannot stop being triggered, but you can lengthen the gap between trigger and reaction—and that gap is where the Holy Spirit lives. Using the latest neuroscience alongside ancient spiritual practices, you will discover how to soothe your nervous system in sixty seconds, how to name your emotions without letting them name you, and how to process pain instead of transmitting it to everyone around you.

Regulate Daily Thinking is the chapter that will turn insight into habit. You will build a daily thought regimen the way people build workout routines—because consistency compounds. You will learn the power of a five-minute morning broadcast that sets the tone for your entire day, the miracle of a nightly thought download that clears mental clutter before bed, and how to use Scripture as a neural pathway rewiring tool. This is where transformation moves from event to lifestyle.

You're Not a Victim comes next, and it is the chapter that will make some religious people nervous—because it dares to say that while you may have been victimized, you do not have to live as a victim. Drawing from the stories of Joseph, David, and Jesus Himself, you will see that refusing the victim mentality is not denying pain—it is denying the enemy the final word over your pain. This chapter will hand you back the pen to your story and teach you how to write "But God..." over every place the enemy wrote "The End."

Mental Toughness follows, and it is where the rubber meets the road. Here you will train like an athlete of the mind (1 Corinthians 9:24–27), learning to endure hard thoughts the way marathon runners endure burning lungs—by keeping your eyes on the prize. You will discover that mental toughness is not the ability to suppress pain but the ability to stay present with God in the middle of pain. This chapter will give you workouts for your soul that will make future storms feel like light rain.

Vision-Driven Thinking is where everything changes trajectory. You will stop living reactively and start living proactively by the power of sanctified imagination. Using Habakkuk 2:2–3 (*"Write the vision and make it plain"*), you will learn to think from the future God has promised instead of toward the past you're trying to escape. This chapter alone has rescued marriages, launched ministries, and healed decades of depression in people who dared to believe God's plans are still good (Jeremiah 29:11).

Feed and Fuel Your Brain is the chapter that acknowledges you are not a spirit floating in space—you are an embodied soul, and your brain needs actual nutrients to host the mind of Christ. Drawing from Daniel's ten-day test (Daniel 1:12–15) and Paul's temple principle (1 Corinthians 6:19–20), you will discover how hydration, omega-3s, sleep, and blood sugar stability are spiritual disciplines in disguise. This is the chapter that will make you close the book, drink a gallon of water, and go to bed at 10 p.m.—and thank me later.

Rewrite Your Inner Narrative is the emotional climax of the journey. Here you will learn that the most powerful story ever told about you is the one you keep telling yourself—and most of us are reciting a horror film when God has already written a redemption epic. Using the science of neuroplasticity and the truth of 2 Corinthians 5:17 ("*If anyone is in Christ, the new creation has come*"), you will systematically replace every lie with God's truth until your inner voice starts sounding like the Holy Spirit instead of your third-grade bully.

Finally, Living as Your Highest Self is the graduation ceremony. This is where you stop managing symptoms and start stepping fully into the abundant life Jesus died to give you (John 10:10). You will learn that your highest self is not an improved version of you—it is Christ fully formed in you (Galatians 4:19). This chapter will show you how to bring your body, soul, schedule, relationships, and dreams into alignment with the person God says you already are in Jesus.

By the time you close this book, you will not be the same person who opened it.

You will have language for the war in your head.

You will have weapons you know how to use.

You will have victories you can point to.

You will have peace that doesn't make sense.

You will have joy that doesn't depend on circumstances.

You will have a mind set free and emotions submitted to the lordship of Jesus.

Most importantly, you will have proof—tangible, daily, undeniable proof—that the same power that raised Jesus from the dead is at work in your thought life right now (Ephesians 1:19–20).

I need to warn you: this journey will cost you. It will cost you excuses. It will cost you the comfort of blaming others. It will cost you the familiarity of chaos. It will cost you the luxury of staying stuck. But what you will gain is everything.

You were never meant to survive your mind.

You were meant to rule it with Christ.

Welcome to the fight of your life.

Welcome to the freedom you were born for.

Turn the page. Your breakthrough is waiting!

INTRODUCTION

CHAMPION *your* THOUGHTS

What are thoughts? We all have them and they travel with us as long as we are awake. We cannot run away from them as they live in us. They are fed by what we see, hear, smell, taste, and touch. They are affected by our emotions, depending on what we are thinking.

Some say we live in the conscious mind and maintain our livelihood are by opinions, beliefs, perceptions, and ideas gathered from the five senses that are part of the hosting of our well-being.

Thoughts allow us to make sense of the world we live in and what we experience. It allows us to interpret what we see, hear, feels, smell, and taste. Thoughts are modifiable elements that we can change with the information gathered from our attitude, belief, environment, experience, skills, and education.

Thoughts are determined through negative and positive thinking patterns which can affect our mental and emotional well-being. Negative thoughts can cause and fill our lives with stress, anxiety, justification, and anger which can become overwhelming to bear.

Positive thoughts do the opposite, they bring us into the light, instead of darkness, and strengthen our mental and emotional health.

We can be in control of our thoughts and can stop them from taking a detour to the destruction of our lives. When a thought comes to the mind, the mind has the choice to store it in its memory depending on how important it is to the person.

If the thoughts are associated with an event of the past that already exists in our memory, then it will stir up an emotion that was registered with that thought. The current thought will become a stimulant that will bring the past thought alive. The memory associated with that emotion will create a world of thoughts that were associated with that past thought creating a web of thoughts, which we find ourselves trapped inside.

As an example, imagine you were walking down the street with your eyes on your cell phone. You were not paying attention to anyone but your phone. In your peripheral vision, your eye picked up a male figure on the other side of the street talking to someone.

You are not really paying any attention, except the fact that he is wearing a red t-shirt. You come home to your spouse or some friends or family member. It's around dinner time, and usually every day there is a routine when you come home.

You may join your spouse, friends, or family to watch a show before dinner or relax with a snack. Most of the time you will all cook together or decide on eating out or ordering in. Your usual routine would be to go to the kitchen to see if food is made and grab a snack.

Today was one of those days you went to the kitchen expecting snacks or a meal. But you notice there is dirty glass in the sink and a few dirty pots and pans on the stove.

This was not unusual, however, a wave of anger rose from the inside and you took the dirty glass and smash it on the floor saying "you have been home all day, why is there nothing to eat and dirty dishes in the kitchen?" Although the routine was not abnormal, there was a burst of anger which was unexpected.

As a psychological assessment is completed, the person getting angry recall his day and his journey home. The only unusual thing that happened that day was man on the opposite side of the road wearing a red t-shirt.

What is unusual about this is the fact that when you were about six years old, you were sexually abused by an older person wearing a red t-shirt that looks similar to what the man was wearing. The figure of the person looked the same, yet you did not pay any attention to the man with the red t-shirt.

A memory card was triggered with an underlining unresolved issue. As the memory card got triggered, anger was released affecting your mental and psychological well-being.

In simple words, we need to resolve unresolved issues, as they can be triggered anytime anywhere like a time bomb as they are retained in mind.

All thoughts revolve around one major thought and are created and developed from the amount of attention we give them. A single thought can expand to multiple thoughts if we don't contain it.

Thoughts feed from any of our sensory nerves, especially what we hear and what we see. They get energy from whatever is connected to our five senses that have relevance to our thoughts.

The dominant thought likes to be the center of attention which will justify every idea that comes to the mind to stay in control and be fed.

We all make decisions consciously or subconsciously without thinking. We all have impulsive reactions when provoked, and depending on the topic, we can even become defensive and rude. We need to give ourselves time to process a thought before impulsively answering, especially when the thought is a trigger to us.

We all have regrets for things we say, mistakes we wish never happened, and the flaws and weaknesses that we present. Although it is difficult to admit it, we are not perfect. Our imperfections are seen through our thought processes and how we vocalize issues and solutions.

When we are able to process any friction or give ourselves time to ponder what we collide with, we will have a better resolution. We will have less stress while cleaning up the mess we created when we allow our minds to think about what we heard and dissect it before concluding how we feel.

Individuals struggling with their mental health reconditions, addictions, and psychological traumas carries multiple thoughts in their mind. Those with addiction issues think of all the reasons to justify their use with the main thought "this will be the last time."

Those with anxiety may struggle from a thought that is triggered by an abusive relationship or a traumatic event. Those with psychosis could have a thought stuck in their mind, and feel pressured to act on the thought, especially if it is being driven by command hallucinations.

Words we hear can trigger an unfavourable memory created in the past. Words have a tendency to look for other words to form a sentence, particularly negative words.

Our brain will search for every word that connects to statements or situations and formulate a sentence. When we have unresolved situations, our brain looks for a vocabulary of words to express feelings.

When we recondition the mind, we gain the power to flush out negative words and experiences, and replace them with positivity. Individuals struggling with depression or a mood disorder only perceive darkness, and as a result, develop a pessimistic approach which leads to hopelessness and suicidal thoughts.

When a person is able to change their thought process and implement positive words, they can turn on the 'optimism' switch in the mind. Nevertheless, every dark room has a light switch, we just need to find it.

Everyone has the power to stop negative thinking from learned therapies. The mind needs to be distracted, even for thirty seconds. For example, during your work hours, you may develop a need to use the washroom and on your way to the washroom, you may meet someone.

You spend about ten minutes talking to them about something and your mind switches the thought of the need to use the washroom to another topic. You may not end up going to the washroom after that conversation as the mind may forget where you were going. However, in a short while, your thought of wanting to go to the washroom will return.

Another example would be driving down the street and smelling food. Although you may have had a meal earlier, the smell of food triggers the brain. Same as seeing someone eat ice cream, someone with a coffee or a burger.

Once our sensory nerves are triggered, we develop urges or cravings. Unhealthy urges and cravings can lead to bigger issues. That's why we need to develop a habit of being able to distract our thoughts even for thirty seconds if we want to rewire the brain. This small habit of processing our thoughts will make a huge difference in our lives.

We could be watching a television commercial advertising a coconut cream pie or fried chicken and suddenly we develop urges or cravings desiring it and want it right away. Just like watching an advertisement for cars, trucks, clothes, and so on.

If we have a buying habit, we will make an online purchase, or head down to the store to satisfy the craving. Several people purchase clothes from window shopping, or what they see others wearing, especially if it is of a popular brand or worn by someone who is a celebrity.

Thoughts are more prominent in the mind just before falling asleep. And, depending on the nature of the thoughts, we could be stuck with a thought or developed racing thoughts.

Thoughts will eventually become like a movie playing in the mind, especially if they are thoughts accumulated during the day by a disagreement or a regret. We have to learn how to manipulate thoughts, creating distractions or diversion thoughts which this workbook will teach.

Thoughts can affect your eating habits, your sleeping patterns, concentration, memory, and other daily functions. They can spiral down into depression and anxiety. We all tend to look for coping strategies that will work quickly, which usually are negative.

Gambling, alcohol, street drugs, misuse of prescription medications, and self-harm are usually the choices for a quick fix. But this workbook teaches other ways that are positive and healthy.

Moreover, you will also learn how to take advantage of your disadvantage and implement strategies that help you to gain control of your thoughts, instead of your thoughts leading you.

Taking control of the thought is the first step to strengthening the mind and re-training your thinking patterns. Positive thinking is the second step to reconditioning the mind and becoming optimistic even in the storms of life.

Re-phrasing what you think or restructuring your thoughts is the third step to bring healing to your emotional life. And, living for what you assume to be fruitful is the fourth step to carry you to be a champion over your thoughts.

We need to champion our thoughts. We need to remind ourselves that champions are not born; they are made. We need to look at ways to become champions over our thoughts in order to conquer our addictions, anxieties, and depression.

Champions use their weakness as strengths, they use their regrets, mistakes, and hurts as fertilizer to fertilize their future, they push hard to overcome their weakness, they strive to win and are not easily distracted, and they are competitive and do not give room for failure.

We need to strive towards being a champion over our thoughts if we want to move out of the pit of feeling low and depressed. We must see the light at the end of the tunnel, the light switch on the wall of a dark room.

We must see the anchor that will sustain us from drifting in the sea of life. We must see the bigger picture of our lives, where we want to be, where we can be, and what would it take to get there.

Champions look at the worse situation that could have happened and remind themselves that there are worse situations than theirs. They look at where they are in life and where they would want to be. They tell themselves exactly what they want to hear. They have mastered the concept of enjoying who they are.

They feel comfortable dating themselves and falling in love with who they see in the mirror. They don't rely on others to add value and worth to their lives, nor are they co-dependent on others.

Champions are confident that life has much to offer if they take the necessary steps to reach their goals.

We are all champions if we chose. It means we need to practice gaining control, train ourselves to be the best, think positively, and be optimistic about life.

When a thought comes that has no bearing of fruitfulness, we should not waste time entertaining them. Some of us may have thoughts including "I feel like a failure," "nobody understands me," and "what's the purpose of my life anyway."

We need to recondition the mind with "I am not a failure," "I don't need others to understand me," "My life has purpose and value" and "I have a bright future waiting for me to discover with family and friends" "I love the gift of life and admire the person I see in the mirror."

We flush our minds with positive affirmations and the tools in this book will help with distractions and diversions to see the value and worth we carry as a person.

Championing our thoughts does not mean that we will have no more negative thoughts. We will be surprised to know negative thoughts are a normal part of our thinking process and even from birth, our brain is hardwired to be more negative as we develop picking up information like a sponge from all those around us.

As we grow up, whatever have tainted the mind, control our thinking and regulates our thoughts. The problem that arise when we failed to control our negative thoughts, is the fact that they consume us mentally, emotionally and psychologically. Our lives become miserable, and we become victim to a number of mental disorders.

Not all mental or psychological issues originates from negative thinking, but they can stem from them. Negative thoughts can be responsible for how we process what we feel without exploring options to be in control.

We need to eradicate all negative thinking before the thoughts consumes us, leaving us bitter, angry, frustrated, and miserable with ourselves.

It can be a challenge to stay positive when life is full of problems that are overwhelming and stress related. differentiate between negative thinking and worries that leads to stress.

We need to program ourselves that negativity will lead us to depressive symptoms and create lack of motivation. It will affect how we function on a day-to-day level at the workplace, with the family, at home and our own personal life.

We will not feel like we could achieve anything and give up without even trying. We will be sad, angry, and exhausted with does not work well together. We will see the entire world around us being the problem than seeing that changes need to come from in the inside out. Some of us may get sick from allowing negativity to percolate like coffee.

We must learn to identify negative thoughts and work towards reconditioning the mind to stay positive, regardless of life's situation. There is always light at the end of the tunnel, be the first to see it.

With a positive outlook in mind, we can gain determination, confidence, and willpower to achieve desired results. Whereas with a negative outlook, even the smallest task seems difficult and a challenge for us to pursue.

Many of us are often afraid of the future developing anxiety. We need to champion the way we think to be in control of not allowing unnecessary thoughts to fill our mind. We are often afraid of the unknown and unsure of what the future holds for us.

This often leads to failure in the mind when there is no motivation to pursue goals. No matter how we look at it, worrying about the future is a waste of time and energy, and it leads to negative thinking. The key to getting rid of these negative thoughts is to acknowledge that there is a limitation as to what we can do and what we cannot do.

The ultimate goal is to focus on taking baby steps and not setting goals that we are unable to meet. This will help avoid unnecessary disappointments.

We all make mistakes from time to time, as we are not perfect. We all have flaws and does things that we have regrets. We all say things we are ashamed of, but people with a negative mindset tend to focus more on past mistakes, flaws, failures and regrets than others.

We have to remind ourselves that we are not perfect and that's okay. When we acknowledge that we have flaws and failures and regrets we wish we can change, we need to work on avoiding making the same mistakes twice.

We want to focus on staying positive and not allowing our minds to go down the rabbit hole where we isolate ourselves from others. We cannot change the past, but we can change the future.

We all have responsibilities in life like everyone else, especially financially. And, in order to grow up and mature we need to take on the responsibility of being financially stable.

There are times when things can go against our financial plans and expectations, creating worry and fear. We have to remind ourselves there are no shortcuts to life. If we don't work hard, we will never have enough money to survive without living from paycheck to paycheck.

We may suffer financial instability when we find it difficult to settle at a job or chose a career path, when there is spending habit, we find difficult to control, lack of resources, and lack of motivation to go back to school and educate ourselves with a proper education.

A lack of financial stability brings negative thinking to the mind as some of us may not be able to past the thought we need to change and not the system. If we believe we can work less and gain more money, we need a plan. We believe in the get rich quick scheme we will soon learn it does not work. If we believe we have a product to see or go on self-employed we need to make sure we understand it may take some time before the business blossom.

We need to convince the mind that we have a blueprint, a plan for our future to avoid financial instability.

We should not allow our confidence level to speak for us and make unwise decisions. Usually lack of confidence can manifest itself in control, frustration and anger. We may think we are never good enough; we cannot do what we put our minds to do, there are more qualities than us and we love hope.

We could be an introvert or extrovert we all can struggle with confidence issues, which leads to negative thinking. We have to mind ourselves that confidence can only grow when we lead the principles of developing our skills, knowledge and experience.

The more we practice our growing in our areas of weaknesses, the more our confidence level will increase. Sometimes we may need to bluff our way in a situation for confidence to manifest itself. You assume you don't have the skills to do the job.

You cannot fulfill your potential. Our lack of confidence can also be responsible for low self-esteem which leads to negative thinking.

Thinking and worrying about something is normal but the real problem arises when this type of thinking becomes continuous. So many of us can be over thinkers, where we may have a bad experience or someone may have said something to us and we hold on to that thought over and over again.

We have to replace negative thoughts with someone positive. We have to remind ourselves that we cannot change a person or what they think, but we can change how we accommodate them. We have to avoid our minds from thoughts that are destructive as the thoughts will become our impulsive thoughts which will be a challenge to break.

Overthinking can result from regrets and wrong choices we made in the past regarding education, career, employment, family dynamics, relationships, marriages, social lifestyles, spirituality, financial and other psychosocial issues.

Moreover, overthinking is believed to be the primary cause of negative thinking resulting in severe mental problems including depression, anxiety and psychosis.

Overthinking can affect our psychological well-being leading to negative thinking and unrealistic expectations.

We all can set unrealistic expectations for ourselves, relationships, family and friends, parenting, career and employment, education, and budgeting. We need to be realistic when we set a goals for our lives.

We need to be realistic otherwise we will become more frustration which leads to negative thinking. Several of us who set unrealistic or unachievable goals find ourselves through processing our thoughts to engage in negative thinking.

We want to avoid losing self-confidence and motivation to become an achiever. We need to focus on that which we know is our destiny for our lives and avoid blaming others for our wrong choices or bad decision we make.

It is very easy to blame ourselves or others when negative things occurs, like spending money and not having enough left over to pay the bills, getting involved in a automobile accident, losing a love one from an unexpected incident.

Very often when something negative happens in our lives we blame ourselves or others instead of accepting the mistake and moving forward. We cannot replace a jar when it falls to the ground and break, so why blame.

Like the old saying "why cry over spilled milk." We need to work on resolutions, otherwise we get the blaming concepts to manifest itself through negative thinking which is manifested through unhealthy choices.

Living a unhealthy lifestyle is really a choice, even though there would not be a lot of people who would not agree. We all love to eat from time to time, and in our western culture we have so many fast food that makes it easy accessible for buy.

Some of us may eat out of convenience when we are hungry and others out of cravings. As much as we can manage our intake of illicit drugs, alcohol, and negativity from others we could also manage unhealthy living.

Unhealthy living is not just wrong choices of food intake, it is the lifestyle we choose to live. It may mean avoiding exercising, socializing, developing spirituality, positive thinking, and the places and things that we are addicted to.

Anything we do that will harm ourselves is considered unhealthy. We need to take pride in who we are and the value and worth we carry as a person. Unhealthy living brings regrets which creates negative thinking.

Our emotions and thoughts can have a significant impact on our physical health and how we function as a person. Living in freedom where we avoid judge it ourselves and others can relief a lot of unnecessary weight on our shoulders.

Negative thinking builds stress and other psychological issues that can weigh us down. It can drain us emotionally where we are like a well without the flow of water. We feel exhausted and find it difficult to relax or even have fun with others.

Furthermore, negative thoughts can influence our relationships, marriages, academic performance, work life, and socializing. They also affects our path to a happy and successful life. Negative thinking affects our psychological well-being.

Fortunately, there are many scientifically proven ways that provide an effective solution to negative thinking which are evidence-based. To live a happy and well-balanced life we have to learn how to dance to the sounds of life.

We need to learn how to recondition the mind and restructure our thinking. We need to flush out the negativity to positivity. There are many tips to do so, however we need to become aware of the change we need to make otherwise it will not happen.

We need to implement changes that will benefit our mental and spiritual wellbeing. We should learn how to catch ourselves and create new neuropathways that are of a positive nature.

It will not be an easy task, but it will be worth it at the end, when others compliment us of the changes they see. When we learn to live happy, calm and peaceful internally, it will manifest itself externally.

We all to learn the healthy stimulants is good for the brain. A change of environment can do this for us. We have to know that it is okay to develop a distance between toxic people and still maintain a relationship with them.

Our minds are fed like our stomach with the environment we live in. It can be what goes on at work, social media we view, the music we listen to, the movies we watch, the news, who we have as role models or blueprints in our lives, and those who influence us.

It's like the dog who had several pops. The dog was hit by a car which left her with a broken leg. She was not helped and walked with a limp. All her puppies walked with a limp as they thought their mother's way of walking was the right way.

Another healthy stimulant is physical activity which helps develop dopamine's and serotonins. Going for walks, the gym, exercising, excursions, tours, getting involved in a sport, running, bird watching, people watching, window shopping, photography, scrapbooking etc.

Anything that involves physical activity will stimulate the brain through the five sensory nerves, releasing dopamine's and serotonins. This is our stress relievers that will help maintain happiness. We need to incorporate at lease thirty minutes a day to something that can involve physical activity, it will help with our anxiety level.

Talk therapy has always been part of human nature. When we talk to someone, we can feel like a weight has left us. It is difficult to find trustworthy people, hence it is important to find therapist.

So many of us struggle to talk about our concerns, our feelings and things that bothers us. Yet talking to someone has helped millions of people around the world. People pay a lot of money to share their thoughts with professionals, where they can empty their mind and find ways to fill it with healthy thoughts.

There are certain people who will come across your life where you can develop a trust to share certain things that bothers you. Nothing is wrong in getting a second opinion.

Sometimes our pride prevents us from talking to others as we believe we have the answer or we know it all. We could never know it all; we could never have the answers to all of the struggles we go through and burying our feelings under the rug will cause us to stumble and fall flat on our faces.

We burn a lot of bridges when we keep everything inside and live a superficial shallow life. Directly and indirectly things that bothers us will only exacerbates if we keep it inside our mind.

We will overthink or we will bury them which will be triggered by others with similar incidents or encounters. Some religious group finds it easy to talk to someone and share their heart, some talk to God, some talk to a friend, some a therapist and others themselves.

We need to talk to someone about deep issues or incidents that has occurred to avoid bigger problems as we age.

Another important healthy stimulant is learning to volunteer our time in humanitarian aid. It is important to do some form of humanitarian work.

People who help others develop a happiness internally with words that they themselves cannot explain. Most hospitals, libraries, shelters, foodbanks, churches, orphanages, and supporting the less fortunate started with volunteers.

Life is about giving, what can we do for others instead of what we can get from others. When we do something for others, we will soon realize that there are others in worse cases than us.

Sometimes we may believe that our issues of life is worse and no one can ever understand, until we start helping others. Feeding the poor, help build a house in a third world country, volunteer at a shelter, give donations to the less fortunate, visit an orphanage, go on a mission trip somewhere and you will be in awe of the problems people deal with. We would appreciate what we have and who we are very quickly.

Learn to be grateful for everything in life, the little things and the big things. The fact that we have life, treat it like there is no tomorrow. Treat others with respect and dignity like today is the last day you will see them.

Developing gratitude and showing how grateful you are will open doors to people's hearts, including yours. Gratefulness keeps us humble and focused on being positive. It's difficult to be grateful and be negative.

When we are fighting negativity, it's easy to forget all the positive things in our lives, making it a challenge to be grateful.

Keeping a journal of our feelings and emotions is a good way to empty the mind. We all should be keeping a log of our day on a journal; this will help with getting rid of negative thoughts. We need to write down our feelings and emotions and how others have impacted our lives in a positive way.

Taking ten to fifteen minutes a day will be like medicine to the soul. Keeping a log will show our progress and will help with a determination of having a healthy thought process.

We would want to generate more positive thoughts than negative thoughts on our notebook, therefore we will become more mindful on controlling what we think.

Mindfulness techniques, meditation, deep breathing, relaxation exercises, and various other self-awareness methods help us to control our emotional reactions to situations. We need to learn how to smell the imaginary rose and blow out the imaginary candle when overwhelmed and is in a anxious mode.

They allow our minds to take over our thought processes. Practicing mindfulness contribute to the ability to use our thoughts more adaptively with fewer negative thoughts.

There are a lot of teaching on mindfulness, meditation, diaphragmic breathing and other self-awareness methods that helps reduce negative thinking.

We need to identify our thoughts in order to rule them out. When we identify our thoughts and note down, we can evaluate their cause for floating around our minds. As we watch our thoughts and identify them, we will be able to regulate them and replace them with positive thoughts.

Although it is not as simple to replace negative thoughts with positive thoughts, identifying the cause of negative thoughts will get us to the root. And, when we can remove the negative roots and replant positive ones, we can have healthy thoughts.

We will need to work on willpower, self-control, and mindfulness techniques to remain calm when we feel triggered with this process. With that being said, some thoughts are activated because we have not put closure to an incident.

It is important to bring closure to incidents or situations that creates negative thinking. There are many ways to bring closure to the past that is affecting the future. We need to replace the negative memory card with positive memory card.

We may need to write down our past on paper and burn it with a celebrate so the brain identifies an ending to the past as a celebration. We would draw the past in an image form in the mind and place them in a mirror, breaking them to pieces where they no longer exist as a whole in image in the mind, replacing the pieces with a new image in the mind.

We could put the past in a bottle and see it float away from you. There are lots of closure suggestions that can be implemented to rid of the negative thinking.

When we chose to do so, we will create new habits that will be healthy, protecting our minds from the battle is goes through from thinking negatively.

New habits are like learning a language or writing with the less dominant hand. It takes time but has positive results at the end. Instead of trying to overcome negative thought patterns, try to replace them with new habits.

We need to turn our attention from harmful thinking to a healthy lifestyle that we can enjoy. Begin with something simple, easy, and most importantly, something you really enjoy that will take your mind off negative thoughts.

A healthy spiritual life is the key to have which can give us insight and wisdom who to target the root cause of issues that are responsible for our mental health.

CHALLENGE *your* THOUGHTS

We need to start a journey of self-reflection and introspection to learn more about our impulsive thoughts and what causes them. You should learn about the interesting world of impulsive thoughts and how they can change your life in big ways to keep your mind healthy.

If we suddenly have an idea, we might act on it right away without thinking it through. They can show up in a lot of different ways, like making decisions on the spot, getting mad for no reason, or doing things without thinking.

These automatic responses can greatly impact our lives, including our mental health, relationships, and overall quality of life.

To deal with our impulsive thoughts in a helpful way, we need to notice and name them when they happen. If we know what makes us act without thinking, we can pay more attention to our thoughts and feelings when things are going on.

We can also learn how our past experiences can change our thoughts by figuring out where our thought patterns came from and how they affect our thoughts now.

We often think about things because of how we feel. They can be very strong triggers that make our automatic reactions stronger and make it harder for us to make good choices. Understanding how emotions and impulsive thinking are connected can help us deal with strong feelings better.

We should think about how important it is to question what we believe and see if it's true. We can be more open-minded and strong in our thinking if we try to see things from other people's points of view.

We should always try to think carefully about how to improve things. We can learn how to handle the good and bad times in life with clarity, wisdom, and emotional health by getting better at not acting on our first thoughts.

We learn a new way to handle thoughts that come to mind quickly as we go through this journey of change together. We need to change how we think and how we see things in our minds if we want to feel better emotionally.

You don't think about the things that pop into your head right away. You might do, feel, or decide things quickly without thinking about them first if you have these thoughts. They happen on their own and can change the way we talk to people, make decisions, and act.

One reason why impulsive thoughts are important is that they happen right away. We don't have a lot of time to think about what they mean or if they're real because they happen so often.

People can act on these thoughts without thinking, like buying something on a whim, taking a risk, or saying something without thinking about how it might affect other people. We can also make snap decisions when we choose people or situations based on our own biases or not much information.

Being able to come up with ideas quickly can change our lives in a big way. They can make people do things they don't want to do, hurt their relationships, and miss out on chances.

If we act on our impulses without thinking about what might happen, we could get bad results or feel bad emotions like guilt, shame, or disappointment.

Coming up with ideas quickly can also change the choices we make. They don't always think things through or use logic, which makes us make decisions too quickly or without enough information.

This can be very bad when you need to think things through carefully, like when you're trying to figure out what to do with your money, your job, or a fight with someone.

Our quick thoughts can also change how well we get along with other people. We might not understand what other people mean, ignore their points of view, or fight with them for no reason when we make quick decisions or act on our automatic thoughts.

People may not get along with each other, which can hurt their relationships and make them miss chances to be nice and understanding.

You need to know what your impulsive thoughts are and how they affect you in order to get them under control. We can begin to learn how to handle these thoughts and change the way we think about them by understanding that they come up on their own and not because we want them to.

By looking into how impulsive thoughts affect us, we can learn more about how they can hurt us and try to find ways to make them less bad.

We need to figure out what makes us have impulsive thoughts before we can change them. Automatic reactions are things you do and think that seem to happen without you having to think about them. We don't think about them much, but they can change our lives in a big way.

To notice when you're having impulsive thoughts, you need to pay more attention to yourself. It means being very aware of how we talk to ourselves and how we feel in different situations. For example, think about how a friend, family member, or co-worker could help you. You might automatically think, "They think I'm incompetent and don't value my work," if you're feeling insecure or scared of failing.

It's helpful to stop and think about how we react to things right away if we want to find impulsive thoughts. You could do this by keeping a journal or writing down your thoughts when you care about something. By paying attention to our thoughts and feelings without judging them, we can learn more about how our automatic reactions work.

Also, watch out for the physical signs that come with having impulsive thoughts. Your heart rate could go up, your muscles could tense up, or you could get a sudden rush of adrenaline. If you know how these feelings work, you can tell when you're having impulsive thoughts.

There are a lot of things that can make someone think about things without really thinking them through. They might be linked to things that happened in the past, things that make them nervous, feelings of insecurity, or certain places.

If someone has been through a traumatic event before, they might suddenly think about it when they are in a situation that reminds them of it. Words or phrases that really get to you can also make you mad.

We can learn about the reasons and patterns behind our automatic reactions by figuring out what makes us act on impulse. This information helps us figure out how to change and question these thoughts in a way that works.

There are usually deeper reasons why we act on impulse that change how we think and do things. We can learn more about why we act on impulse and how to deal with these reactions better by looking into these roots.

We do things without thinking about them a lot of the time because of what we've learned and how we've grown up. The things we do and where we grew up affect how we think and act. We might have learned to do what the people in charge say right away and follow the rules if we grew up in a strict and authoritarian home.

We might have thought it was okay to act on impulse or that it worked because we had seen it praised or rewarded before.

People expect us to act a certain way most of the time. When we see someone not doing what they should, it can make us act without thinking. We might do something without thinking if we think that people are judging or criticizing us for not following the rules of society. This is to keep us safe or get their permission.

When we act on impulse, our beliefs and values can also change how we act. These strong beliefs change how we see ourselves and the world.

When we put getting what we want right away or our own safety above everything else, we are more likely to act on impulse. People might think these things because of their culture, biology, or things that have happened to them.

Some mental health problems can also make people act on a whim. Impulsivity is a key symptom of conditions such as attention deficit hyperactivity disorder (ADHD) and borderline personality disorder (BPD).

These conditions may arise from a convergence of genetic, neurological, and environmental factors, increasing our vulnerability to impulsive thoughts and behaviours.

It's important to think about how our feelings affect us when we're trying to figure out why we do things on a whim.

Our thoughts and actions are greatly affected by how we feel. When we're scared, mad, or excited, we might not think about what we're doing before we do it. If we know what makes us feel a certain way and learn how to control our feelings, we can stop ourselves from acting on impulse.

You need to look at how different things work together to understand why people act on impulse. There are many things that can make us act or think on impulse, such as how we were raised, what we learned, our social and cultural influences, our core beliefs, our mental health, and how we feel.

We can find better ways to deal with and change our automatic reactions when we learn more about what causes them. We can slowly lessen the effects of impulsive thinking and make more rational and thought-out choices by doing things like self-reflection, therapy, and personal growth.

When we act on impulse, our past experiences still have a big effect on how we think, act, and respond. When we have sudden thoughts, we should think about what happened in the past that made us feel that way.

You can change how you think and do things without even thinking about it based on what has happened in the past. People who have experienced a lot of bad or traumatic things may begin to have negative thoughts about life. You might say things like "the worst will happen" or "I know what happened without thinking of other options" when you think this way.

The way a person was raised and what happened to them as a child can also make them more impulsive. People who grew up in a place where their opinions were always ignored or invalidated may have thoughts of self-doubt that come to them quickly or always need other people to agree with them.

These ways of thinking can change how people make decisions and cause them to act on impulse to get quick approval or validation.

People can also think quickly when they have failed or had a setback in the past. Someone who has been let down or turned down a lot might be scared of failing or feel like they need to do something quickly without thinking about what could happen.

You might want to take risks or make choices without thinking them through when you're scared.

We can better understand how we react without thinking by learning how events in the past change the way we think about things.

By figuring out what experiences have shaped our thoughts, we can start to question and change them in a more helpful way.

One good way to do this is to go to therapy or do exercises that make you think about how the things that have happened in the past have changed how you think now.

This process can help us find beliefs from their past that are harmful or hold them back. Once we know what these beliefs are, we can start to change them by looking for proof that they aren't true.

We can learn more about why we think things without thinking by looking back on things that have happened to us.

With this information, we can improve ourselves and our ability to think clearly and logically. It helps us let go of the past and make better decisions based on what's going on now instead of just reacting to what happened before.

Using logic to change how we think and react automatically is a great way to do it. It means examining the fundamental concepts and convictions that result in impulsive thought processes and substituting them with more rational and equitable alternatives. Cognitive restructuring helps us think more clearly and make better choices.

Cognitive restructuring is about figuring out how you act and think in different situations without really thinking about it. You need to know how you think and pay attention to it for this to work.

If we pay close attention to our thoughts, we can start to figure out what beliefs and assumptions are behind our impulsive reactions.

After you know what these automatic thoughts and beliefs are, the next step is to see if they are true. This means looking at the evidence that supports these ideas and considering other possible explanations and perspectives.

You should carefully check to see if these ideas are true and fair, and if they are based on facts or twisted views.

"Gathering evidence" is a helpful way to change the way you think. This means getting proof that either backs up or goes against your automatic thoughts and beliefs.

We can see how true our first answers were by looking at how strong and reliable this evidence is. This process helps you get rid of cognitive biases and see things more clearly and fairly.

We can also use logic to change how we react without even realizing it. This means checking our thoughts for logical errors or cognitive distortions, such as making broad generalizations, jumping to conclusions, or thinking the worst. We can stop thinking in these wrong ways by asking ourselves questions and coming up with more realistic and logical ones.

You should get rid of the automatic thoughts that come to mind and replace them with new ones that are more balanced. One way to do this is to think of different ways to talk about or understand what's going on.

We can learn more and be more open-minded if we look at things from different angles. This process helps us figure out how likely it is that good things will happen, what we can do to make them happen, or other ways to look at the problem.

Cognitive restructuring also means working on and strengthening the new rational thoughts. You need to do it over and over again and be consistent to make the new ways of thinking stronger.

We can learn to question our automatic reactions and replace them with thoughts that are more balanced and make more sense over time.

Learning how to think logically is a key step in fighting off impulsive thoughts and changing how you act without thinking.

Because their brains are wired to be biased, people often have thoughts that come to them quickly. They can get them to do and believe things that don't make sense. If we work on having a mind that is more rational and balanced, we can make better choices and control our impulsive thoughts better.

Learning how to find and question cognitive distortions is one of the best ways to make your thoughts more rational. Cognitive distortions are things we do every day that change how we think. Cognitive distortions include black-and-white thinking (seeing things as either all good or all bad), overgeneralization (making broad conclusions from little evidence), and personalization (taking too much blame for things that aren't our fault).

When we find out about these lies, we can start to doubt their truth and replace them with thoughts that are more fair and true.

To think clearly, you need to know the difference between facts, guesses, and opinions.

Automatic thoughts come from our brains based on what we know and how we feel. These ideas might not be true and might be very personal. We can find out more about what's going on by carefully examining the evidence and looking for other explanations.

We should ask ourselves questions like, "What proof do I have to back up this idea?" and "Is there another way to explain what's going on?"

To think more logically, you need to be open-minded and willing to change your mind. It means being aware that our initial thoughts and evaluations are not always accurate or comprehensive.

We can better understand a situation and stop ourselves from acting on our first thoughts if we look for and think about other points of view. One way to do this is to use techniques like "perspective-taking," which means trying to see things from the other person's point of view.

To improve your logical thinking, you should also work on your critical thinking. This means being able to look at information without letting your feelings get in the way, find flaws in logic, and figure out how reliable and accurate sources are.

We can question our quick thoughts and think about them in a more logical and reasonable way when we use critical thinking. A big part of this process is asking questions like, "What evidence supports this idea?" and "Is this idea based on facts or guesses?"

You need to put in the time and effort to learn how to think more clearly and fairly. If you work hard and think about yourself, you can get better.

If we question our impulsive thoughts and change how we automatically react, we can have more control over how we make decisions and live lives that are more fulfilling and meaningful.

In our daily lives, we often believe things and guess about them without really checking to see if they are true. These automatic thoughts can make you act on impulse because they might not have all the facts, be biased, or be based on memories that aren't true anymore.

If you have thoughts or feelings that make you act on impulse, you should stop and think about what you really believe. People often have strong beliefs that change how they think and act without them even knowing it.

By questioning our assumptions, we can find out if they are true and if our brains are playing tricks on us.

It can be helpful to figure out what thoughts or beliefs are making us do things without thinking if we want to start questioning our assumptions. These thoughts could be things you say to yourself, things you think about, or pictures in your head that go with the bad behaviour. We can look at these automatic thoughts more closely once we find them.

To find out if our automatic thoughts are true, we can look for proof that they are and proof that they aren't. This means looking at the facts and coming up with other ways to understand or explain what's going on. This process helps us see things more clearly and stop our impulsive thoughts from taking over.

It's also important to pay attention to how our automatic thoughts change how we feel. It's hard to think clearly and make choices when we feel something. We can tell if our impulsive thoughts are right for the situation we're in right now by being aware of and understanding the feelings that make them happen.

You can also ask other people if you think your ideas are wrong. Talking about our automatic thoughts and beliefs with people we trust can help us come up with new ideas and see things in a different way. People can change how we think by giving us new ideas or facts that we hadn't thought of before.

We can also think about who we are and what we've done. If we take the time to think about our own cognitive biases, preconceived ideas, and past experiences, we might be able to spot patterns or trends that make us think quickly. If we pay more attention to ourselves, we can get rid of these biases and think more clearly.

We can learn more about ourselves and the world by asking ourselves what we think we know. When we act on impulse and do something about it, we can learn more about the cognitive biases and distortions that affect how we think. By going on this journey of self-reflection, we can learn how to be more fair and clear-headed. This will help us feel better and make better decisions.

It's very important to look at things from different points of view when you want to change how you react automatically and question your impulsive thoughts. If you have a narrow or biased view of the situation, you might think of things on the spur of the moment. If we look at things from different angles, we can learn more about what's going on.

Thinking about how other people see things is one way to get a different point of view. This means getting other people's opinions and feelings about the situation, even if they don't agree with you.

Listening to what they have to say can help us learn more about ourselves and question any biases or assumptions that might be affecting our impulsive thoughts.

You can also think about your life and yourself. This means taking a step back from the strong emotions that come with impulsive thoughts and looking at the situation from a more objective point of view.

We can figure out what's going on in a new way by asking ourselves what we think we know and looking at other possible reasons.

You can also get information from other places. There is a lot of information and a lot of different kinds of media these days. We should be careful about where we get our news and look for other points of view.

We can learn more about what's going on by looking at it from different points of view and questioning our own biases.

It's important to remember that looking for other points of view doesn't mean giving up what we believe or what we care about. But it's a way to learn more and come up with other things you could do. This process can help us be more open-minded and willing to change how we think about things. It makes us question how good our quick ideas are.

To really look for other points of view, you have to be curious and want to learn. This means being willing to hear new ideas and learning how to talk to people who don't agree with you. Reading books from other cultures or talking to people who don't agree with you might also help you feel more empathy and understanding.

If you want to change how you think and act quickly, it's a good idea to see things from other people's points of view. By looking at things from different angles, thinking about other ways to understand them, and actively looking for different points of view, we can see the world in a more balanced and nuanced way.

This process helps people grow, learn how to think critically, and be more understanding. This helps you make choices that are better and more logical.

A lot of the time, impulsive thoughts come from making quick decisions and acting on instinct without thinking them through. You need to learn how to solve problems that make you think in order to stop acting on impulse. This is how we can get through hard times and make better decisions.

Recognizing that your first thought might not be the best one is the first step in solving a problem. It could mean not doing what you thought at first and instead using your brain to figure things out.

First, you need to figure out what the problem is. If we can clearly explain the problem, we can stop acting on impulse and focus on finding the right answer.

Once you know what the problem is, you need to get all the facts you need. This means gathering information, processing it, and considering the situation from various perspectives. It takes time to learn about the situation, but doing so helps us understand it better, which can help us come up with better and more informed answers. It also helps to question any thoughts or biases that might make you change your mind at the last minute.

You can use critical thinking to come up with possible answers if you know a lot about the problem and how it works. You need to use your imagination and come up with a lot of different ideas. We can see a lot of different points of view and outcomes when we think about a lot of different things.

You should hold off on making a choice right now and be open to all possible answers, even if they seem strange or go against what you first thought.

Being able to think critically is a big part of this process of evaluating. It's important to think about how each choice could help or hurt you and other people. You need to stay calm and think clearly while you do this. Don't let your heart or mind get in the way.

Don't let short-term gains make you change your mind. Instead, you should look at the pros and cons of each choice without bias and think about how it will affect the future.

You can choose the best one after looking at all of them closely. Choose this based on your beliefs, goals, and the results you want. You might have to make a deal or find a solution that works for everyone. When we think critically, we make better choices. This means that we don't just do things because we want to or think they are right.

The last step in solving a problem is to do what you said you would do. You should make a list of what you need to do and any problems or challenges that might come up. A good plan keeps us on track and focused, which means we are less likely to get sidetracked by random thoughts or things that come up.

It's important to know what's going on around you and inside you when you're trying to figure something out. If you think about what you say and do every day, you might be able to change any patterns of acting on impulse.

We can slowly get rid of our impulsive thoughts and make better, more balanced choices by using our problem-solving and critical thinking skills on a regular basis.

Learning about impulsive thoughts has shown us how many things can affect our lives. We now know that making decisions on the spur of the moment can have a big effect on our health and the choices we make. By recognizing their presence and effect, we have taken the first step toward getting back in control and living a life with more meaning and purpose.

Learning to notice automatic responses has been a big part of our journey. We know what makes us think on the spot, and this helps us keep them from taking over our lives. Now that we know how we usually act, we can plan and think about how to respond better.

We have changed since we started to think about why we do things without thinking. We have thought about our past to figure out what makes us act on impulse. We have learned a lot about the patterns and triggers that keep impulsive thoughts going by thinking about ourselves and looking inside ourselves. This lets us change and question these ideas.

We can see how our past experiences change the way we think by looking closely at them. We have used this chance to heal old wounds, let go of beliefs that hold us back, and change how we see things. We can grow as people and have a better, stronger future by looking at our past in a new way.

It's clear that how we feel can change how we see things. We have learned how to deal with the complicated relationship between feelings and acting on them without thinking, since feelings can make it hard to think clearly. We can now deal with tough situations more clearly and logically because we know ourselves better and can control how we feel.

Cognitive restructuring has been shown to successfully alter the operation of automatic responses. We have examined the veracity of our impulsive thoughts through a rational lens. By consciously questioning and changing our automatic reactions, we have given ourselves the power to adopt more balanced and constructive points of view.

We have changed a lot because we can think clearly. We have learned to think critically and logically, which helps us see things clearly and without bias. We can now make better choices and deal with life's problems with more strength and wisdom because we accept reason.

We have opened up new doors by questioning what we think we know. We have come to see the limits of our automatic thoughts and beliefs by carefully examining their truth and considering other points of view. We have welcomed different points of view by making it a place where people are open-minded and curious.

We have learned how to deal with sudden thoughts by using our problem-solving skills. We have used critical thinking to come up with new ways to avoid and fix problems.

We have learned new ways to do things, gotten stronger so we can deal with problems, and changed our minds to be more open to growth and strength.

As we finish this chapter, let's be happy with how far we've come in questioning our quick thoughts. We have changed how we respond automatically, which has given us back control of our lives, helped us grow as people, and made our lives more meaningful and purposeful. We are now better equipped to deal with the problems that life throws at us. We should accept this new information and keep moving toward a life full of choices that are mindful, decisions that are empowered, and peace of mind.

MASTER *your*
EMOTIONS

We need to look into the deep world of emotions and see how they can change us when we think about "Championing Your Thoughts and Mastering Your Emotions." Our emotions are like a colourful tapestry that runs through our lives every day, changing how we think, what we do, and how we feel overall. When we learn how to understand and control our feelings, we can make amazing changes in our lives.

Negative feelings can be hard to deal with. We need help understanding what these feelings are and how to deal with them so we can get over them. We need to become more aware of and control our emotions, which helps us find balance within ourselves.

Being nice and understanding is a strong force that can make a big difference in our own lives and the lives of others. We need to learn how to grow these traits in ourselves, which will help us feel more connected to other people and have better relationships.

Being thankful and having strong positive feelings can make our lives happier and more fulfilling. How we handle anger and frustration can help us feel better.

Fear and anxiety can be very strong at times, but we can learn how to get rid of them. Building emotional resilience is an important part of our emotional health because it helps us get through hard times and face life's problems head-on. We can handle the complicated world of emotions with grace if we work on our emotional intelligence.

When we work on our emotional intelligence, we become more aware of ourselves, more understanding of others, and better at talking to people. We know that our relationships and emotional ties have a big effect on our lives. By strengthening these connections, we build a network of people who support us and help us grow. When we change how our brains work to use our emotions, we open up a world of endless possibilities.

Emotions are like bright colours that fill in the empty spaces in our lives. They change how we see things, make choices, and interact with the world. They are a big part of what makes us human and help us learn about our inner world.

To use the power of emotions to make changes, you first need to know how they work in your life. Our feelings are like a compass that tells us what is most important to us and helps us choose what to do. They tell us a lot about what we want, need, and care about.

For instance, being happy could mean that we are doing things that make us happy, while being sad could mean that we need to think about things or make a change.

We learn a lot about ourselves when we pay attention to how we feel, and we can make better choices that are more in line with who we really are.

Our feelings are also very important in our relationships and how we talk to other people. They are a universal language that lets us connect with other people on a deep level.

For instance, empathy is based on how well we can understand and relate to how other people feel. We can connect with other people better when we learn to understand our own feelings. This makes our relationships stronger and our connections healthier.

Emotions can change how we think and feel, and they can also help us learn how to control them. Our feelings can change how well we remember things, pay attention, and figure things out. People who are grateful and happy are more creative, more able to bounce back from setbacks, and generally happier with their lives.

On the other hand, stress or anger that lasts for a long time can be bad for our mental and physical health. To fully understand how important emotional mastery is in our daily lives, we need to become more aware of our emotions and learn how to control them.

This means learning to be interested in our own feelings instead of judging them. We learn a lot about what makes us feel the way we do and how our feelings work when we watch and think about them. This helps us respond in better and more helpful ways.

When we have bad feelings, they can feel like a heavy weight on our shoulders, which makes it hard to see things clearly. But if we know how to use the right tools, we can recognize and deal with these feelings, which will help us take back control and see life in a more positive light.

Before we can deal with negative emotions properly, we need to know what causes them and what they are for. It's normal to feel sad, angry, scared, or frustrated in different situations in life. They can show needs that aren't being met, point out areas where you can grow, or act as a way to protect yourself.

We can be more understanding and curious about these feelings if we learn more about them. Recognizing negative emotional patterns is an important first step in learning how to deal with them and take charge of our feelings.

Through self-reflection and mindfulness, we can learn to identify negative emotions that recur and the triggers associated with them. We can stop our feelings from getting out of hand if we know how we feel.

Acceptance is a powerful method for managing negative emotions and mastering emotional regulation. It means letting our feelings be and not judging or fighting them. We can make a safe space for self-exploration and growth by being honest with ourselves about how we feel.

This exercise helps us get past our first emotional response and look for solutions that will help us. Finding healthy ways to deal with bad feelings is important for learning how to control our emotions and get better at them.

Negative thoughts can make you feel bad. We need to challenge and alter these thoughts, substituting them with more constructive and beneficial ones. If we change the way we think, we can turn bad feelings into chances to grow and feel stronger.

Being kind to ourselves is a big part of controlling negative emotions and learning how to deal with our feelings. We need to learn how to be kind and understanding to ourselves so that we can accept our flaws and mistakes without judging ourselves.

Self-compassion is a strong base for emotional health and helps us deal with bad feelings with strength and kindness. When we learn how to recognize and deal with bad feelings, we get back the power to change how we feel.

With the tools and information we have, we can learn how to turn bad feelings into things that help us grow as people. This will make your life happier and more complete. Being aware of our feelings and learning how to deal with them is another way to learn how to control them.

We have basic skills that help us handle our emotions in a smart and graceful way. Being emotionally aware means being aware of the little things that our feelings tell us. This helps us learn important things about what's going on inside of us.

We learn more about ourselves when we learn more about our feelings. This helps us figure out what makes us feel the way we do. It is the ability to recognize, understand, and embrace our emotions as they arise.

To cultivate emotional awareness, it is imperative to create an environment that fosters mindfulness and reflection. This means taking the time to notice how our feelings affect our bodies, minds, and hearts.

Meditating, writing in a journal, or just taking some quiet time to think about ourselves are all ways we can watch our feelings without judging them. This lets us gently explore their depths and learn from what they are trying to tell us.

Emotional regulation is the conscious management and modulation of our emotions, which is the same as being aware of our emotions and mastering them. We can deal with our feelings in a way that fits with our goals and values when we know a lot about how we feel.

Mindfulness is a great way to keep your feelings in check. Mindfulness helps us notice our feelings in the present moment without judging them, as we talked about before. This lets us see them without worrying too much about how strong they are. Mindfulness helps us put some distance between our feelings and our actions, which lets us make better, more balanced choices. We need to learn how to handle stress in a good way.

These are things we do and activities that help us deal with our feelings in a good and helpful way. Exercise, relaxation techniques, talking to trusted friends or professionals, or doing creative things like writing, art, or music are all good ways to deal with stress.

Emotional intelligence is the ability to recognize and understand not only our own emotions but also the emotions of others. This is part of becoming more aware of and in control of our emotions. We become better at understanding and feeling what other people are going through when we work on our emotional intelligence. This helps us keep our emotions in check and get along well with others.

To learn how to control our emotions and become more aware of them, we need to be kind, caring, and patient with ourselves. We should not try to be perfect; instead, we should see our feelings as important messengers that help us grow and feel better. When we learn how to be aware of and control our feelings, we can face the problems in our lives with strength, grace, and honesty.

Learning how to be more kind and understanding. These deep traits can unite people, dismantle barriers, and foster a more compassionate and harmonious society.

When we show empathy and compassion, we not only feel better ourselves, but we also make the world a better place for other people. Putting yourself in someone else's shoes and seeing the world through their eyes is what empathy is all about. It is a skill that helps us understand, accept, and help others more deeply.

When we learn to be empathetic, we break down the walls of judgment and criticism. This means being nice to others and accepting that their experiences are different from yours. Compassion is the real wish to help people who are hurting. It goes beyond just understanding; it also means doing something good.

When we care about others, we can help those in need by being kind, giving them a hand, and supporting them. It makes us want to change the world, one small act of kindness at a time.

To learn how to be kind and understanding, we need to get to know ourselves better first. This will help us control our feelings. When we understand our own feelings and experiences, we can better understand how other people feel and what they need. It helps us develop a strong sense of empathy by understanding the struggles and successes that make people who they are.

To be empathetic and compassionate, you need to listen actively. When we truly listen to someone without judging or cutting them off, we give them a safe space to say what they want to say. Accepting their feelings and experiences helps us feel like we belong and are connected, which makes the ties that bring us together stronger.

Empathy and compassion extend beyond personal relationships; they encompass the wider community and beyond. We can be more compassionate by doing nice things, volunteering, or giving money to good causes. It reminds us that we are all connected and that we can make the world a better place by changing the lives of others.

What we do has an effect on the people around us, making them want to be like us. This is how we make a ripple effect of kindness that changes our neighbourhoods and makes the world a kinder and more understanding place.

When we practice empathy and compassion, we not only learn how to control our emotions, but we also help ourselves grow and make the world a better place. Positive feelings are like sunshine that makes us feel better, lifts our spirits, and makes our lives better. They can change how we see things and make us feel happy and content all the time.

To foster positive emotions, it is crucial to develop mindfulness of the present moment. We often get so busy with our daily lives that we forget about the present and instead think about our past mistakes or our future goals. But when we focus on the here and now, we can see and feel all the beauty and wonder that is around us.

Being thankful is a strong feeling that can change us in a big way. It looks like a bright flame. It means being aware of and grateful for all the good things in our lives, no matter how big or small. Being thankful makes us more aware of how rich our lives are, which makes us very happy and satisfied.

Keeping a gratitude journal can help us feel thankful. We write down the good things and blessings in our lives every day and think about them with deep gratitude. We can cultivate a mindset of abundance and gratitude by writing down what we have instead of what we lack.

Saying thank you to others is a great way to make yourself feel good and get better at it. By thanking and recognizing others for their help and kindness, we build stronger relationships and a culture of gratitude.

A heartfelt thank-you note, a kind act, or a sincere word of thanks can make us and the people around us feel better. Another good way to keep good feelings going is to do things that make us happy and fulfilled. These activities can be anything from spending time outside, being creative, or doing something you like to do with people you care about.

We can have times of pure happiness and satisfaction by making sure to do these things on purpose. When we start to feel grateful and happy, our lives will start to change a lot. Positive feelings help us deal with stress and problems, which makes us better at handling them. It helps our relationships with other people when we show happiness and thankfulness.

If we work at it and are intentional, we can make our lives full of happiness, satisfaction, and a constant sense of gratitude. Enjoy every moment and fill your heart with gratitude and positivity to begin this life-changing journey.

We need to learn how to deal with anger and frustration if we want to control our emotions. Everyone has these feelings from time to time. These feelings can be very strong, but they can also hurt you if you don't know how to deal with them.

We need to change how our brains work to deal with anger and frustration. You can use anger and frustration to help yourself grow and change by using techniques and strategies that turn them into positive forces.

It's very important to be aware of yourself when you're mad or upset. If we know what makes us feel this way, how it usually happens, and how it feels in our bodies, we can stop it before it gets worse. If we can see the early signs of anger and frustration, we can do things to deal with them in a healthy way.

A big part of dealing with anger and frustration in a good way is learning how to talk to people. When our needs aren't being met or when our relationships are having problems, we often feel this way. If we learn how to communicate assertively, we can talk about our worries and feelings in a calm and polite way. This will help people understand and figure out what to do.

We need to learn how to calm down and keep our feelings in check. When you're angry or upset, taking a moment to stop, breathe deeply, and do something calming like meditation, writing in a journal, or working out can help you feel less angry or upset. This helps us think more clearly and calmly, which helps us make better choices and solve problems.

You can deal with anger and frustration in a good way by learning how to be empathetic and see things from other people's points of view.

Putting ourselves in other people's shoes and trying to see things from their point of view can help us be more kind and open-minded.

Understanding the real reasons behind our anger and frustration can help us figure out what we really need and want. Sometimes, these feelings are hiding deeper feelings of pain, fear, or insecurity.

By addressing and resolving these underlying issues, we can diminish the frequency and intensity of anger and frustration in our lives. Being proactive about solving problems can help you turn your anger and frustration into positive action.

Instead of letting these feelings fester and lead to bad behaviour, we can use them as motivation to find and fix the real problems. This positive attitude lets us think of new ideas and make our lives better.

To deal with anger and frustration in a good way, we need to be patient, practice, and be willing to grow as people. You will never stop learning about yourself, thinking about yourself, and mastering yourself.

Changing how we feel about these feelings can make our lives happier and more peaceful, and it can also make our relationships and health better. We don't have to let our anger and frustration take over.

Instead, we can use their fiery energy to make ourselves and the world around us better. We take charge of our lives and open ourselves up to endless chances to grow and change when we deal with these feelings in a positive way.

We also need to learn how to deal with fear and anxiety. They can be hard to deal with, but with the right tools and attitude, we can get through them and feel better about ourselves. This will help us take charge of our thoughts.

Negative self-talk and distorted thought patterns are often the cause of fear and anxiety. Cognitive restructuring is the process of finding and questioning these bad thoughts and replacing them with more realistic and positive ones.

By consciously changing the way we think, we can slowly change the way we think and feel less scared and anxious. If you are scared or anxious about certain things or situations, it can help to slowly and carefully put yourself in those situations. Start with small steps and gradually increase how much you see over time.

By facing our fears over and over again in a safe and controlled way, we can desensitize ourselves and become more sure of our ability to handle things. You can deal with fear and anxiety better if you learn and use relaxation techniques.

Deep breathing, progressive muscle relaxation, guided imagery, and meditation are some ways to calm our minds and bodies and make anxious and fearful feelings less strong. When you have intrusive or negative thoughts that make you feel scared or anxious, the thought-stopping technique can help.

When we have a thought that isn't helpful, we can mentally shout "Stop!" or picture a stop sign. Then, on purpose, replace that thought with a picture that calms you down or a positive statement. We can better handle fear and anxiety when we learn how to control our feelings.

Identifying and naming our feelings, learning how to calm ourselves down, and doing things that make us feel better and relax can all help us deal with tough feelings. It's important to learn how to be nice to yourself when you're scared or worried.

We should be nice to ourselves and remember that these feelings are normal for everyone. When things get hard, we should talk to ourselves in a positive way and take care of ourselves. When you need help or support, don't be afraid to ask for it. When fear and worry get too much, it can help to do things that take our minds off of them for a while.

Do things you like, spend time with people you care about, be creative, or work out. These good distractions can help us focus on something else and take our minds off of our worries.

Another way to learn how to control our feelings is to build emotional resilience. It means being able to change and get back on your feet after hard or stressful times. It means being able to handle your feelings, stay positive, and solve problems in a healthy way.

Building emotional resilience is good for our mental health and well-being as a whole because it helps us handle life's ups and downs better and with more emotional stability. There are a few key things you can do to make yourself emotionally stronger.

First and foremost, you need to know yourself. This means knowing and understanding how we feel, what we think, and what makes us angry. Knowing how we feel can help us understand how we act and react in different situations.

This self-awareness is what lets you build emotional strength. It can be very helpful to talk to people who make you feel safe, understood, and cared for when things are hard or stressful. To build emotional strength, it's important to have a good attitude.

Believing that we can get through tough times and staying positive can really help us get stronger emotionally. This means changing the way you think about bad things, focusing on the good things and what you're good at, and being grateful. We can become stronger and better able to deal with problems if we work on having a positive attitude.

Building emotional resilience is very important for your mental health and well-being. We can get better at handling tough times and coming out on top by knowing ourselves, building a support system, learning how to deal with stress, and staying positive.

It takes time, effort, and self-reflection to build emotional resilience, but the long-term benefits for your emotional health are worth it.

Resilience helps us get back on our feet when things go wrong. We can be stronger by changing how we think about bad things, looking for solutions instead of problems, and asking for help when we need it.

Every day, take some time to think about how you feel, how you treat other people, and how you've changed as a person. Consider how you could have improved in certain situations and what lessons you can derive from them.

We need to strengthen our emotional ties in relationships in order to control our feelings. Building and keeping strong emotional ties in our relationships is good for our health and happiness.

We feel like we belong, supported, and happy when we have meaningful relationships with other people. Emotional support strengthens the emotional bonds in relationships. It means being there for people when they are having a hard time and cheering them on when they win.

It takes compassion, understanding, and a desire to help and comfort others. We can show how much we care about the relationship and make our emotional ties stronger by being understanding and listening.

To make emotional connections, you need to spend time together that is meaningful. It means paying full attention to the other person. This could mean doing things or talking about things that both people enjoy, which would create memories and experiences they can share.

The relationship gets stronger and more important when you spend quality time together. Saying thank you and doing small things for others can really help strengthen emotional ties. You can show that you care and make the relationship stronger by doing simple things like offering to help, saying thank you, or surprising the other person with something they value.

Learning to control your emotions is a journey that can change your life and make you very happy. The first thing you need to do to make your inner world peaceful is to learn how your feelings affect your daily life. We can deal with life's problems with clarity and wisdom when we accept and understand all of our feelings. Recognizing and dealing with bad feelings is a useful skill that helps us get through hard times with strength and grace. Being aware of ourselves and using healthy ways to deal with stress can help us turn negative feelings into chances to grow and get better. When we know and control our feelings, we can choose how we react to things that happen to us and around us. We can find more emotional balance and stability by being mindful and thinking about ourselves. This helps us stay positive even when things are hard.

Being nice and understanding to other people is good for our mental health and our relationships. We spread kindness and positivity when we try to understand and help others. This makes us feel more connected. Being grateful and taking care of our good feelings are great ways to feel better and stay healthy. We can make our lives happier and more positive by concentrating on the good things and being grateful for even the little things.

Learning how to deal with anger and frustration in a good way can help us grow as people and make our relationships better. We can keep our boundaries healthy and build bridges of understanding and cooperation by learning how to express and channel these strong feelings in healthy ways.

You need to be strong and brave to get over fear and worry. It is a big step toward making your life better and happier. We can get over our fears and worries by questioning our limiting beliefs and using helpful coping strategies. This opens up a lot of doors for growth and new experiences.

Building emotional resilience is a lifelong process that teaches us how to bounce back from setbacks and handle life's problems with strength and grace. We can be stronger by taking care of ourselves, having a growth mindset, and building a strong support system. It takes a lot of time and effort to get better at emotional intelligence.

You have to learn about yourself and get better all the time. If we get better at understanding and controlling our feelings, putting ourselves in other people's shoes, and talking to them, we can deal with relationships and the complexities of life more easily and honestly.

Building stronger emotional ties in relationships is also an important part of good mental health. When we work hard to build strong relationships with the people we care about, we create a support system that helps us through the good and bad times in life.

Remember that it takes time, kindness to yourself, and regular practice to learn how to control your feelings. If we use the ideas and strategies in this chapter every day, we will start a journey that will make us feel better and make our lives more fulfilling and happy. Take this trip to heart, and may your new emotional skills bring you peace and happiness for the rest of your life.

REGULATE *your*

EMOTIONS

Being able to understand, talk about, and control our feelings in ways that make us feel good, connect with others, and be strong is called emotional regulation. Don't try to hide how you feel or pretend to be fine. It's about learning how to respond instead of react and respecting your feelings without letting them control you. When done with care and understanding, emotional regulation can help people heal and make their relationships stronger.

Emotions are a part of what makes us who we are. They talk to us, help us, and put us in touch with other people. Emotions such as happiness, sadness, anger, fear, love, and shame are not arbitrary; they are indicators. They tell us what hurts, what matters, and what makes us feel better. But when we feel too much or too little, it can change how we see things and make it hard for us to get along with others.

Kathleen and I have seen every kind of feeling in our family. Because we have seven kids, our house is like a living lab for how to show feelings. There have been happy days and sad days. One night, one of our kids cried because they got into a small fight. They were worried about school. It wasn't just the problem; it was everything else that was happening. That moment reminded us that emotional outbursts usually have deeper reasons.

There are many reasons why people get too emotional. Problems can happen because of changes in hormones, differences in the nervous system, or genetic predispositions. It can also be psychological, like stress that lasts a long time, trauma that hasn't been dealt with, or needs that aren't being met. And sometimes it's about relationships—people not being there for you, not being able to talk to you, or being in bad places.

Trauma is a big part of emotional dysregulation. When someone has been abused, neglected, or lived in constant fear, their nervous system becomes very alert. They could get really mad about little things or stop working completely. Ford (2017) says that trauma makes it harder for the brain to control emotions. People might avoid things, get too excited, or feel like their feelings are too much for them to handle.

People who are addicted also handle their feelings differently. People often use drugs to feel better when they're in pain or to get away from strong feelings. But over time, they mess up the brain's natural ways of keeping things in order. People can go from being very happy to very angry or very sad and not be able to calm down. Norvilitis and Mao (2013) discovered that emotional instability frequently correlates with impulsive behaviours, including drug use.

Some people, on the other hand, have trouble showing how they feel. This could be because of cultural conditioning, fear of being vulnerable, or past experiences of being turned down. We have seen that keeping your feelings to yourself can make you feel alone in our family.

One of our kids stopped talking about how they felt after being made fun of at school. They needed time, safety, and a calm presence before they could talk to them again.

It's good for your mental health to be able to say how you feel. It helps us talk to other people, deal with our feelings, and let go of stress. The Bible says the same thing. The book of Ecclesiastes says, "***There is a time to cry and a time to laugh.***"

There are many feelings in life. David's psalms are very honest about how he feels, whether he's angry, sad, happy, or hopeful. He didn't keep his feelings to himself; he told God how he felt.

But you need to find a way to balance how you say what you think. Unfiltered outbursts can hurt relationships. If you keep things to yourself for a long time, you may get depressed. Emotional regulation is the middle ground; it's the ability to feel a lot and do the right thing.

Some feelings are more likely to get too big. Anger can help you hide your pain, fear, or frustration. If they don't keep it in check, it can make them angry or pull away. When you re anxious, threats seem bigger, and you start to worry and stay away from them. If you don't talk about or deal with your sadness, it can become hopelessness.

When you feel ashamed, you want to be by yourself and feel bad about who you are. Euphoria, especially when it comes to addiction, can turn into a dangerous high that makes people lose touch with reality.

There is a reason for each of these feelings. Anger draws lines. When something is wrong, anxiety tells us. Sadness makes you think. Shame is a sign that you're getting better. Euphoria is a way to show how happy you are. But you should pay attention to these feelings when they take over or change. To be able to control your feelings, you need to know what they are, accept them, and do something about them. You can improve and learn how to do it over time.

First, you need to give the feeling a name. Say exactly what you mean, like "I'm sad," "I'm worried," or "I'm too busy." Giving things names makes them less scary and easier to understand. Taking a break before doing something lets you think about how you feel.

Taking a deep breath, counting to ten, or walking away can help you change how you feel. You might be able to find deeper needs or memories from the past when you think about the source. You can learn more by asking, "What's really going on?"

You should be able to safely express your feelings. Writing in a journal, talking to a friend you trust, praying, or doing something creative can all help you deal with stress. You should also treat yourself well. You get stronger emotionally when you tell yourself nice things like "It's okay to feel this" or "I'm doing my best."

One of the grounding techniques that can help you stay in the present is to use touch, sound, or movement to connect with the present. You can find new ways to think about things and get help through therapy, support groups, or spiritual guidance.

We have made up family rituals to help us deal with our feelings. During "feelings check-ins," everyone talks about one feeling they had that day. We don't say "You always..." anymore; instead, we say "I feel..." We believe that writing in a journal, praying, and spending time alone are all good things to do. These things have helped us and our kids become stronger emotionally.

People who have been through trauma need safety, time, and help to learn how to deal with their feelings. Your nervous system may be more focused on keeping you alive than on connecting with other people. The first step to getting better is to be there for someone. Ford (2017) says that mindfulness, breathing, and fixing relationships are all good skills-based ways to deal with trauma.

We have walked with people we care about who are very hurt on our journey. After years of emotional abuse, one family member found it hard to trust their own feelings. They started to get their voice back with therapy, prayer, and constant support. It wasn't easy to learn how to control your feelings; it took a long, holy time.

Addiction can help you forget about how bad you feel. Getting better means being able to feel things again without running away, numbing, or overreacting. If you want to get better, you need to learn how to control your feelings. It helps people deal with pain, meet new people, and make good choices.

We've helped friends get better, and we've seen how being able to control your feelings can change your life. "I used to drink when I was nervous," said one friend. I breathe, pray, and call someone now. It's true, even though it's hard. That honesty is at the heart of emotional control: bravery, connection, and growth.

People can control their feelings better in safe places. Homes, workplaces, churches, and communities can help or hurt mental health. Being safe means being seen, heard, and treated well. It means helping people without trying to change them and letting them feel things without judging them.

We try to make our home a safe place for feelings. We let them in, set limits, and talk about how we feel. We say, "It's okay to cry" and "Let's talk about it." These short sentences teach people how to trust each other and how to control themselves.

Being calm all the time isn't what emotional regulation is about. It's about staying in touch with God, yourself, and other people. It's about not letting your emotions control you while still respecting them. It's about figuring out how to care about people and make good choices.

This chapter should make you want to look after your mental health. Emotional regulation is a way to find peace, whether you're dealing with addiction, getting over trauma, or just learning how to name your feelings. We learn how to be more graceful, make friends, and be honest with ourselves through it.

TRIGGERED **EMOTIONS**

When Kathleen and I think back to the years of raising seven children, we often laugh at how naïve we were at the beginning. We thought parenting was mostly about teaching kids how to behave, how to do chores, how to succeed in school. What we didn't realize was that parenting would expose every emotional trigger we had buried inside. It was as if God had given us seven mirrors, each child reflecting back something about ourselves we hadn't yet faced.

One of my earliest lessons came when our oldest was about nine years old. She had a habit of muttering under her breath when she didn't like what I said. One evening, after I told her to finish her homework before watching TV, she rolled her eyes and whispered something I couldn't quite catch. My blood boiled instantly.

I raised my voice, lectured her, and sent her to her room. Later that night, I sat alone in the living room, replaying the scene. Why had I reacted so strongly? It wasn't just about homework. It was about respect. Growing up, I often felt dismissed, and that old wound was triggered by my daughter's eye roll. That was the moment I realized my emotional hot button wasn't really about her—it was about me.

Kathleen had her own triggers. She grew up in a home where her father was stern, and her mother carried the weight of keeping everything together. Chaos unsettled her deeply. So when our house erupted into noise—seven children arguing, toys scattered, dishes piled high—Kathleen felt overwhelmed.

I remember one Saturday morning when the kids were chasing each other through the kitchen, spilling juice and knocking over chairs. Kathleen froze, tears welling up. She wasn't just frustrated with the mess; she was reliving the instability of her childhood. Identifying that trigger helped us both. Instead of blaming the kids for "making her upset," we began to see the deeper story behind the emotion.

The Bible became our compass in those moments. Psalm 139:23 says, *"Search me, O God, and know my heart; test me and know my anxious thoughts."*

That prayer became our lifeline. We asked God to show us the roots of our reactions, to reveal the anxious thoughts that fueled our anger or fear. Slowly, we began to see that emotional triggers were not enemies to be avoided but invitations to grow in grace.

One of the hardest lessons was learning the difference between reaction and response. I'll never forget the night our teenage son came home past curfew. My first instinct was to react—slam the door, raise my voice, and ground him for a month. But James 1:19 echoed in my mind: *"Everyone should be quick to listen, slow to speak and slow to become angry."*

I took a breath and asked him why he was late. His answer humbled me. He had stayed behind to help a friend who was struggling with drinking and was depressed. My anger melted into gratitude. If I had reacted, I would have crushed his willingness to share. By responding instead, I preserved trust. That night taught me that mastering emotions is not about suppressing them but about directing them toward life-giving outcomes.

Kathleen often reminded me, "Our kids don't need perfect parents. They need parents who respond with grace." That became our mantra.

Of course, grace didn't always come easily. There were mornings when spilled cereal, missing shoes, and sibling squabbles collided into chaos. I remember one particular morning when we were already late for church. One child couldn't find their shoes, another spilled milk across the table, and two were fighting over who got to sit in the front seat. I felt the pressure rising in my chest. My voice was about to explode. Instead, I stepped into the bathroom, closed the door, and whispered, "Lord, give me patience." That thirty-second pause changed everything. I walked out calmer, and the kids noticed. They didn't see a perfect dad, but they saw a dad who was learning to master his emotions.

Jesus modeled this for us. Luke 5:16 says, ***"But Jesus often withdrew to lonely places and prayed."*** When crowds pressed in and disciples misunderstood Him, He didn't lash out. He withdrew. He regulated His emotions by anchoring Himself in communion with the Father. That example became our blueprint.

Kathleen discovered the power of breathing exercises. When tension rose, she would take three slow breaths, inhaling peace and exhaling frustration. She taught the kids to do the same before exams or difficult conversations. I remember watching our daughter before a trumpet recital. She was nervous, hands trembling. Kathleen knelt beside her and said, "Let's breathe together." Three slow breaths later, our daughter walked on stage with confidence. Breathing became more than a technique—it became a way of inviting God's peace into the moment.

Grounding helped me personally. When I felt overwhelmed, I would notice five things I could see, four things I could touch, three things I could hear, two things I could smell, and one thing I could taste. It brought me back to the present moment. Mindfulness, for us, was not just psychological—it was spiritual. Psalm 46:10 says, "*Be still, and know that I am God*." Stillness reminded us that God was in control, even when emotions felt like storms.

Pressure came in many forms: financial strain, health scares, teenage rebellion, endless laundry. Staying calm under pressure was not natural—it was learned. One story stands out. Our third child had a medical emergency. Panic surged in me, but Kathleen's calm steadied the room. She prayed aloud, her voice firm yet gentle. That calmness became contagious. Even the doctors noticed. Philippians 4:6-7 became our anchor: "*Do not be anxious about anything, but in every situation, by prayer and petition, with thanksgiving, present your requests to God. And the peace of God… will guard your hearts and your minds in Christ Jesus*." Calmness under pressure is not the absence of emotion—it is the presence of peace.

Yet emotional triggers often pointed to deeper wounds. For me, the wound was rejection. Growing up, I felt overlooked by teachers and adults in general. So when my children ignored my instructions, it touched that old scar. Kathleen carried her own wounds—her father being a school teacher and she was the youngest. Chaos reminded her of the instability she felt then. Healing came through prayer, counselling, and honest conversations. We learned that wounds don't disappear by ignoring them. They heal when exposed to the light of Christ. Psalm 147:3 says, "*He heals the brokenhearted and binds up their wounds*." That promise became real for us.

Processing past pain meant revisiting memories we would rather forget. It meant acknowledging how those experiences shaped our triggers. One evening, Kathleen shared with the kids about her childhood. She explained how it made her crave stability. The children listened, and suddenly they understood why she valued order so deeply. That vulnerability built bridges. Processing pain is not weakness—it is courage. It allows us to break cycles so our children don't inherit the same unhealed wounds.

Forgiveness became the cornerstone of our emotional journey. Parenting seven children meant countless apologies—both given and received. I remember snapping at one of the kids during a stressful morning. Later, I sat down and said, "I'm sorry. Daddy was wrong to speak harshly." That apology released healing. Acceptance meant recognizing that emotions are part of being human. Jesus wept in John 11:35. He felt anger in Mark 11:15.

Emotions are not sins; they are signals. Emotional release often came through prayer. Sometimes Kathleen would journal her frustrations, then pray over them. Sometimes I would go for a walk, talking to God aloud. First Peter 5:7 says, *"Cast all your anxiety on Him because He cares for you."* That casting was not a one-time act— it was daily, sometimes hourly.

Looking back, we see that emotional triggers were not obstacles— they were opportunities. They taught us patience, humility, and dependence on God. They shaped our children too, showing them that emotions can be managed, wounds can be healed, and forgiveness can flow freely.

Parenting is sanctifying. It reveals our hot buttons, but it also reveals God's grace. And in the end, we find that the journey of emotional growth is not just about raising children—it is about being raised ourselves, into the likeness of Christ. Championing our thoughts and mastering our emotions is not a destination; it is a lifelong journey. It is the daily choice to pause, to breathe, to forgive, and to trust that God is at work in the midst of our mess.

YOU'RE *Not A* VICTIM

We are not victims. When pain is fresh, trauma echoes through our thoughts, or addiction makes it hard to see clearly, that truth may seem far away. But it is still true.

What happened to us does not define us. What we do with it is what makes us who we are. The moment we begin to see our suffering not as a sentence but as a starting point, we begin to reclaim our power.

In our family, Kathleen and I have faced seasons that tested our strength. Raising seven children has brought joy, but also moments of deep emotional strain.

One of our children struggled with depression after a traumatic experience at school. Another wrestled with anxiety so intense it led to panic attacks. And we, as parents, carried our own burdens—memories of childhood wounds, financial stress, and the quiet ache of wondering if we were doing enough.

There were nights when we sat together in silence, holding hands, praying for peace. And slowly, we began to understand: healing doesn't come from denying pain. It comes from transforming it.

A victim mindset tells us that we are powerless. It convinces us that our circumstances are in control. It whispers that we are broken, that we are stuck, that we are alone. But that is a lie.

We are only victims when we allow our situation to rule over us. The moment we choose to rise, to reach out, to believe in change—we begin to reclaim our lives.

Whatever we submit to becomes the lord over our lives. If we submit to fear, fear will govern our decisions. If we submit to shame, shame will shape our relationships. But if we submit to hope, to healing, to truth—then those become our guides.

Scripture echoes this in Romans 6:16: *"**Don't you know that when you offer yourselves to someone as obedient slaves, you are slaves of the one you obey**?"*

Emotional slavery is real—but so is emotional freedom.

Trauma, PTSD, addiction, anxiety, and depression are not signs of weakness. They are signs that we've lived through something hard. Judith Herman (2015) writes that trauma shatters the sense of self, but recovery restores it.

That restoration begins when we stop seeing ourselves as victims and start seeing ourselves as survivors. Survivors who are learning, growing, and becoming.

The brain is not fixed. It is capable of change. Neuroplasticity—the brain's ability to form new neural pathways—means that even after trauma, we can rewire our minds.

We can create new habits, new thoughts, new beliefs. We can move from fear to courage, from despair to hope. According to Doidge (2007), the brain changes in response to experience. That means every time we choose healing, we are reshaping our future.

Kathleen began journaling during a season of depression while living in Croatia. At first, it was just a few lines a day. But over time, it became a lifeline—a way to process, to pray, to reflect.

One of our children started painting as a way to express emotions they couldn't speak. That art became a mirror of their healing. I began walking every morning, using that time to breathe, to think, to reset. These small acts were not dramatic, but they were powerful. They were ways of saying, "I am not a victim. I am choosing life."

We must use our negative situations as fertilizer for our future. Pain can become purpose. Struggle can become strength. The very things that tried to destroy us can become the soil in which we grow.

When we share our stories, when we help others, when we build something beautiful from the ashes—we become a "better me."

Mental toughness is not about being hard. It's about being resilient. It's about feeling deeply and still choosing to move forward. It's about falling and getting back up. It's about saying, "This hurts, but I'm not done." Developing mental toughness means practicing self-compassion, setting boundaries, seeking support, and staying committed to growth.

Sometimes we use the victim mindset as an excuse not to progress. We say, "I can't because of what happened." But healing begins when we say, "I can, even though it happened." That shift is powerful. It opens the door to possibility. It invites us to dream again.

We need each other. Healing is not a solo journey. We need safe people, wise mentors, loving friends, and compassionate professionals. We need community. In our family, healing has come through conversations, prayers, shared meals, and quiet moments of presence. It has come through therapy, through church, through laughter, and through tears.

We must see ourselves as champions, winners, overcomers. We must believe that we have something to offer. That our lives matter. That our healing is not just for us—it's a blueprint for others. When we rise, we show others that rising is possible. When we heal, we give others permission to heal. When we live with purpose, we become a light.

You have the ability to rewire your mind. You can create new neural pathways. You can overcome the victim mindset. You can develop mental toughness. You can become the person you were meant to be—not in spite of your pain, but because of how you've transformed it.

This journey is not easy. But it is sacred. Every step you take toward healing is a victory. Every time you choose hope over despair, connection over isolation, truth over lies—you are reclaiming your life.

You are not a victim. You are a survivor. You are a champion. You are a blueprint for others. You are becoming a "better me."

MENTAL TOUGHNESS

There are a lot of different ways and methods that Mental Toughness can help you build and improve your mental strength. If you do these things, you'll be able to deal with life's problems and challenges with a positive attitude and a strong will.

Not everyone is born with mental toughness; it's a skill that can be learned and improved over time. It helps you handle problems, bounce back from failures, and do well when things change. You can use the power of your mind to find the strength to get through hard times and do well in every area of your life.

To better understand mental toughness, we need to look into the mental strength that will help us do well in any situation. It will give us the tools and information we need to build a strong and positive mindset, which will help us face problems head-on and keep going even when things get tough.

Remember that getting mentally tough is something you have to keep doing. You have to be dedicated, practice, and promise to improve yourself. Be open to new ideas and ready to change as you work on your mental toughness. With each step you take, you'll find the amazing strength inside you. This will help you get through hard times, reach your goals, and be happy.

Being able to recognize and fight negative self-talk is one of the most important parts of being mentally tough. What we say to ourselves in our heads can have a big effect on how we feel, how we act, and how healthy we are in general. We can change how we see ourselves by changing negative self-talk into positive and empowering affirmations.

Negative self-talk often takes the form of self-criticism, doubt, and limiting beliefs that stop us from reaching our full potential. It stops us from growing and can have a big effect on how good we feel about ourselves and how confident we are. We can start to change our brains for the better, though, if we are aware of these negative thought patterns.

We can fight and replace negative thoughts with more positive and helpful ones when we realize that we are talking to ourselves in a bad way. We need to change how we see things and learn to be nice to ourselves as part of this process. Instead of being hard on ourselves for things we think we did wrong or didn't do, we can choose to be kind and understanding.

Change is something we all have to deal with, and to become mentally tough, we need to accept it with an open and positive mind. We need to learn how to accept change and be more flexible, and how these traits can make you mentally stronger in general.

We can grow, learn more about ourselves, and become better people when things change. When we accept change, we open ourselves up to new ideas, experiences, and ways of looking at things. Instead of being afraid of or fighting change, we can choose to see it as a chance to move forward and grow.

One of the most important things to do to build mental toughness is to understand that change often brings uncertainty and the unknown. It requires us to be willing to leave our comfort zone and go to places we've never been before. We grow as people and become stronger by doing this because it gives us new opportunities and helps us get better at what we do.

Being open to change is the same as being able to adapt. It's being able to change and do well in different situations, even when things are always changing. A mentally strong person can change what they think, plan, and do to fit the needs of a situation that is always changing.

We get better at handling problems and setbacks when we learn to be flexible. We don't get angry or stressed out when things happen that we didn't expect. Instead, we see them as chances to learn, grow, and think of new things. This way of thinking keeps us positive and in charge, even when things get tough.

Also, being open to change and learning to be flexible can help you feel better about yourself and your abilities. We learn to trust ourselves more as we deal with new problems and get through them. This confidence gives us a strong base for our mental toughness, which lets us face future problems with unshakable determination.

Having a growth mindset is one of the best things you can do to be mentally strong. A growth mindset means that you really believe you can get better at things and learn new things if you put in the effort and are willing to do so.

People who think this way see problems as chances to grow and failures as steps toward success. By having a growth mindset, we can reach our full potential and open ourselves up to a world of possibilities.

When you have a growth mindset, you don't see failures as things that will always get in your way. Instead, you see them as chances to learn and grow. People who have a growth mindset don't let failures get them down. Instead, they look at them with interest and strength.

They see problems as puzzles to figure out and setbacks as temporary roadblocks on the way to their goals. They see problems as opportunities and mistakes as lessons that will help them grow in the future.

One of the best things about a growth mindset is that it can change how we see our own skills and potential. We know that intelligence and skills can change over time when we have a growth mindset. This knowledge lets us break free from the limits we put on ourselves and lets us learn and grow all the time.

When we have a growth mindset, we are more likely to try new things that are outside of our comfort zone. We need to understand that taking a risk on the unknown can help us grow as people and in our jobs.

Being willing to push your limits and try new things makes you stronger and more adaptable, which are important traits for dealing with the ups and downs of life.

People with a growth mindset also have a positive view of hard work and not giving up. People who have a growth mindset don't think of hard work as a chore; they think of it as an important part of growing and doing well. They know that if they work hard and practice on purpose, they can become experts in any field they choose.

You also love learning when you have a growth mindset. It makes people want to learn, try new things, and ask for feedback and criticism that is helpful. People's constant desire to learn helps them grow in both their personal and professional lives, and it gives them the strength to reach their goals.

You can learn and get better at having a growth mindset over time. Be nice to yourself and have a positive, patient attitude about how you're growing. Celebrate the small wins and the progress you've made. They are steps toward your bigger goals.

Setting goals that are realistic is an important part of getting mentally tough. It means making a plan to get what we want to happen. Setting clear, doable goals helps us succeed and keeps us going by giving us a positive attitude.

When we set goals, it's important to find a balance between being realistic and being ambitious. It's good to push ourselves, but if we set our goals too high, we might get frustrated and lose motivation if we can't reach them. Setting realistic goals makes us feel like we've done something, which gives us a boost of energy and keeps us motivated and positive.

On the way to reaching our goals, we will have problems. These problems can show up in a lot of different ways, like when things take longer than expected, when you doubt yourself, or when you have trouble with other people. But we can get through these problems and keep working toward your goals if we learn to be mentally tough.

Remember that the path to success is not always a straight line. There will be problems, detours, and delays that come up out of nowhere. But we can get through these hard times and come out stronger than ever if we have a positive attitude, set realistic goals, and are mentally strong enough.

Perseverance, or the strong desire to keep going even when things get tough, is a great trait that can help us succeed and grow as people. Perseverance is a strong trait that can help you become mentally tough in a good and encouraging way.

Staying positive even when things are hard is one of the most important things you can do to build mental toughness through perseverance. Sometimes it seems like things are too hard, but if we work on having a positive attitude that looks for solutions and learns from mistakes, we can stay positive even when things are tough. We become more sure of ourselves and better at dealing with new problems as we solve each one.

In today's fast-paced world, stress and anxiety are becoming more common. But when it comes to making ourselves mentally stronger, we see these problems as chances to learn and get better. We can handle stress and anxiety well, which gives us the strength and grace to face the problems that life throws at us.

It's normal to feel stressed and anxious about the demands and unknowns of everyday life. They are signals from our bodies and minds that we need to take care of ourselves and pay attention to them. We can turn these experiences into chances to grow as people and build the mental strength we need to do well in any situation if we look at them in a positive light.

To build mental toughness, it's very important to take care of our physical, emotional, and mental health. A self-care routine that makes us stronger should include things that make us happy, being aware of our surroundings, and getting enough sleep.

Two very important traits that make you mentally strong are self-efficacy and confidence. When we are very sure of ourselves, we think we can do things and succeed. Self-efficacy, on the other hand, is the belief that we can do things or reach goals. They work well together and help us deal with problems and make the most of opportunities with a positive attitude.

We need to look after ourselves and do things that are good for our minds, bodies, and spirits. Taking care of our bodies and minds makes us feel better about ourselves and raises our self-esteem. Be nice to yourself, do things that make you happy, and accept yourself as you are. Taking care of ourselves will boost our self-esteem and confidence.

Building confidence and self-efficacy takes time and work, and it doesn't happen all at once. As we start using these strategies in our daily lives, we will see a big change in how we see ourselves and what we can do. If we have a strong sense of self-efficacy and confidence, we will be able to face challenges with strength, take advantage of new opportunities, and reach our goals with unwavering determination.

In today's fast-paced world, where everyone is always on their phones, being able to focus and concentrate is a very useful skill. You can learn and get better at this skill with hard work and a good attitude, which is a good thing. We can use strategies and techniques to help us stay on task and concentrate, which will make us more productive and successful.

When we work on our focus and concentration, we open up a world of new possibilities. Imagine being able to work on something without any distractions or interruptions. If we work on this skill, we can get to a flow state where time flies by and we get a lot done. It makes a big difference when we can really focus, whether we're studying for a big test, working on a hard project, or doing anything else that needs our full attention.

Creating the best possible environment is a great way to help you stay focused and on task. Find a clean, uncluttered place to work that doesn't have anything else in the way. To help us focus on the task at hand, turn down the noise from outside and make the space comfortable. We tell our minds to focus and get rid of things that could get in the way by making a special place for focused work.

Managing our time well is another good way to get things done. Break up our work into smaller, more manageable parts and set aside certain times to work on them.

Try using the Pomodoro Technique, which says to work in short, focused bursts and then take short breaks. This not only helps us stay focused, but it also keeps us from getting tired or burned out. If we keep practicing, we'll be able to focus for longer periods of time and get a lot more done.

A positive attitude is important for improving focus and concentration, along with things outside of yourself. Be interested in and curious about what you're doing. Be excited about it and eager to learn more about it. When we work on having a good attitude, we build an inner drive that helps us stay focused and concentrated, which makes the experience more enjoyable and rewarding.

Remember that it takes time and work to get better at focusing and concentrating. Celebrate the small victories along the way and remember that every step forward is a step forward. Every time we work hard, we are building the foundation for a focused and concentrated mind that will help us do well in all areas of our lives.

We are getting ready for success and reaching our full potential by getting better at this skill. We need to let go of our intense focus and get great results in everything we do.

Meditation and mindfulness are two very powerful tools that can change our lives. We can build a strong and positive mindset, feel better emotionally, and be more determined to face challenges by making these habits a part of our daily lives.

Being mindful means being fully present and engaged in the present moment without any judgments or attachments. It means not thinking about the things that are bothering us in the past or the future and instead enjoying the richness of the present moment. Being mindful makes us very aware of what we're thinking, feeling, and sensing in our bodies. This lets us choose how to respond to them instead of letting them control us.

Meditation, on the other hand, is a specific practice that includes a number of different ways to calm your mind, find peace within yourself, and get to know yourself better. It can help us calm down and clear our minds if we focus on something, like our breath.

Take some time every day to be quiet and think about yourself. Be open and interested in what's going on right now. We will discover the profound potential within ourselves and a newfound strength that will guide us toward a life of resilience, purpose, and joy.

To sum up, we've looked at a few different ways to develop a strong and positive mindset. We have given ourselves the tools we need to deal with problems, get over obstacles, and do well in all areas of life by using these methods.

We began by understanding how important it is to stop negative self-talk and get stronger during tough times. We learned how important it is to be open to change and adaptable, as well as how important it is to have a growth mindset. Setting realistic goals and overcoming challenges became important parts of our journey, as did using the strength of perseverance.

We also talked about how to handle stress and anxiety, how to feel better about yourself and your abilities, and how to stay focused and concentrate better. All of these things make us mentally stronger and give us the strength and grace to deal with life's ups and downs.

We looked into how meditation and being mindful can have a big impact on your life. By making these things a part of our daily lives, we learned how to stay calm and strong, deal with stress, become more aware of ourselves, and have a kind relationship with ourselves.

Remember that getting mentally strong is a process that never ends. You need to work hard, practice, and want to get better. Let's use what we've learned in this chapter in our daily lives as we move on. Let's look at the problems we have as chances to learn and get better. When things go wrong, let's be patient with ourselves and celebrate even the smallest steps forward.

When you work on your mental toughness, you don't have to be perfect or never have problems. It's about building the inner strength and resilience you need to get through hard times, get back on your feet after a failure, and do well when things are uncertain. It's about changing the way you think so that you see problems as chances to learn and grow. It's about changing how our brains work.

We should keep using what we've learned and what we know. We should have faith in our minds, trust in our abilities, and know that we can handle anything that comes our way.

Mental toughness gives us the strength to keep going, the ability to bounce back, and the will to reach our goals and be happy. We need to be sure of ourselves, strong, and have a new goal in mind. We can be mentally strong because we know we can handle anything that comes our way.

REGULATE daily

THINKING

Our minds are full of thoughts all day, from the time we wake up until the time we go to sleep. Some research indicates that individuals generate tens of thousands of thoughts daily. A lot of these thoughts go by quickly without us noticing, but some stick around and change how we feel, what we do, and even our future. The danger lies not in the quantity of thoughts we possess, but in those we permit to remain unaddressed. Unchecked daily thoughts can turn into seeds of negativity, triggers of trauma, and patterns that take us away from peace and purpose.

I have learned through my own journey that we can't ignore our daily thoughts.

When I first moved to Canada, I realized that I needed to be able to control my thoughts as well as my body in order to stay alive. I wouldn't have made it through the cold winters, the long hours in the tobacco fields, or the loneliness of living in a barn if I had let despair take hold. Every day, I had to question my thoughts and turn fear into faith, doubt into hope, and negativity into purpose.

The same lesson applied to my marriage and family life. Living with Kathleen showed me that thoughts that aren't controlled can easily turn bad. My mind would make flaws or weaknesses seem bigger than they were if I thought about them too much. If I let my irritation grow, it could turn into anger. If I let my disappointment last, it could turn into anger.

I had to learn to stand up for my thoughts every day and question them before they became harmful. I remembered the words of 2 Corinthians 10:5: "*We demolish arguments and every pretension that sets itself up against the knowledge of God, and we take captive every thought to make it obedient to Christ.*" That verse became a daily habit for me: I took control of my thoughts, refused to let them run wild, and made them obey Christ.

Thinking negatively has effects. It can bring back old wounds and trauma from the past. It can change how things really are, making small problems seem huge. It can ruin relationships by turning love into fighting, trust into doubt, and unity into division.

I have seen how letting your thoughts go can make you angry, explode, or rage. I know how easy it is for regrets and mistakes to turn into bad habits if you don't challenge them.

But I have also seen how powerful it is to question your daily thoughts. I stop negativity from growing when I choose to face it. I bring back peace when I tell the truth instead of lies. When I read the Bible, I keep my mind on hope. Philippians 4:8 says, "*Finally, brothers and sisters, whatever is true, whatever is noble, whatever is right, whatever is pure, whatever is lovely, whatever is admirable—if anything is excellent or praiseworthy—think about such things.*" This verse tells us to protect our minds, choose what we think about, and fill our daily thoughts with good and worthy things.

There were times when being a parent really put me to the test. Kathleen and I had different styles, and our disagreements could have easily led to fights. Every day, I had to question my thoughts and remind myself that our differences were not weaknesses but chances to help each other. I had to fight the urge to dwell on my anger and instead think about the bigger picture: raising kids with love and faith. *"**Train up a child in the way he should go; even when he is old he will not depart from it**"* (Proverbs 22:6) helped me remember that the goal was not to prove who was right, but to lead our children in the right direction.

When I traveled to Croatia during the war, I had a lot of bad thoughts that almost took over my mind. The regrets, mistakes, and bad decisions all made my mind go crazy. I kept going back to the past, blaming myself, and feeling bad. I learned to fight those thoughts by focusing on God's promise in Isaiah 43:18–19: "***Forget the former things; do not dwell on the past.***"

After investing our lives in Croatia during the war from 1994-1997 Kathleen and I were missionaries pastoring a church and helping the community. We went through several hardship including the death of a close friend of mine. There are a lot of mistake made, wrong choices and regrets as we were only in our early twenties. Always bittersweet memories.

*"**Look, I'm doing something new!**"* Those words made me remember that God isn't limited by my past mistakes; He is always doing something new. To champion my thoughts, I had to let go of regret, accept forgiveness, and believe that God could turn even my mistakes into lessons for growth.

Thinking every day is powerful. It can change how we feel, what we do, and what happens to us. But it needs to be questioned, protected, and directed. "***Above all else, guard your heart, for everything you do flows from it***," says Proverbs 4:23.

To guard the heart, you must first guard the mind. If we don't pay attention to negative thoughts, they will affect what we do, what we say, and how we interact with others. But if we question them, give them the truth, and ground them in scripture, they will lead to peace, purpose, and change.

Every day, I learn this lesson again. I have to fight for my thoughts every day, from the little things that bother me to the big things that weigh me down. I need to fight against negativity, face lies, and tell the truth instead. I need to protect my mind, keep my emotions in check, and make room for learning and growing emotionally for the rest of my life.

It's true that thoughts that aren't paid attention to can be dangerous. They can cause trauma, make people angry, and break up peace. But the power of thoughts that are challenged is stronger. They can mend wounds, bring back hope, and change lives. And so every day I choose to fight for my thoughts, to take them captive, to make them obey Christ, and to fill my mind with things that are true, good, right, pure, beautiful, and worthy of praise.

That is the way to be the best version of myself. That is the practice that keeps growth going, changes mistakes into lessons, balances emotions, and grows compassion. That is the discipline that keeps things from getting out of hand and making people angry. And I will learn that lesson every day for the rest of my life.

Our minds are busy all the time. Scientists think that a person has tens of thousands of thoughts every day. Most of them don't last long, but some do and change how we feel, act, and even see ourselves. The problem isn't how many thoughts we have; it's how many we don't pay attention to. A belief can change a person's fate, and a thought that isn't checked can turn into a belief. That is why I have had to learn, and am still learning, to stand up for my daily thoughts.

There were times when I was very negative. It could be something small, like being annoyed with Kathleen for a habit that bothered me, or something bigger, like feeling bad about the choices we made when we went to Croatia during the war. If I didn't question those thoughts, they would turn into anger, resentment, or hopelessness. I had to learn to stop them before they got worse. The Bible helped me remember this discipline. The Bible says in 2 Corinthians 10:5, "*We take captive every thought to make it obedient to Christ.*" I made that verse a part of my daily life. I had to control my thoughts and not let them go wild. I had to bring them under Christ's authority.

This lesson came to me in a very real way through marriage. Living with Kathleen meant learning how to look past flaws and weaknesses. In the beginning, I tended to focus on the little things that bothered me. My mind would make them seem bigger than they really were. If I hadn't learned to stand up for my ideas, those little annoyances could have turned into anger. But I remembered 1 Corinthians 13:4–5: "*Love is patient, love is kind... it is not easily angered, it keeps no record of wrongs.*" To champion my thoughts, I had to choose patience over anger, kindness over criticism, and forgiveness over resentment.

Championing my thoughts meant not getting caught up in the little arguments and instead looking at the big picture. Small annoyances almost made me angry at times. If I hadn't questioned my thoughts, any of these things could have made me angry: a fight with Kathleen, a disappointment with the kids, or a problem at work. James 1:19–20 reminded me that "*everyone should be quick to listen, slow to speak, and slow to become angry, because human anger does not produce the righteousness that God desires.*"

To champion my thoughts, I had to slow down, listen, choose patience, and not let anger control me.

Another important lesson was how to balance my feelings. Feelings are strong; they can make you feel good or bad. I had to learn how to control them instead of letting them control me. Proverbs 25:28 says, "*Like a city whose walls are broken through is a person who lacks self control.*" I didn't want to be a city with no walls. I wanted to be strong, safe, and protected. That meant learning how to control myself, how to balance my feelings, and how to respond with wisdom instead of acting on impulse.

I learned that every experience, good or bad, was a chance to learn. Every fight taught me how to be patient. Every error made me more humble. Every time I regretted something, I learned to forgive. Every problem taught me to have faith. I learned to see each day as a lesson and life as a school. Emotional expansion meant letting myself grow, stretch, and become more than I was before. It meant learning to love deeply, forgive freely, and feel deeply. It meant getting better at being kind, understanding, and caring.

I learned from all of these experiences that supporting daily thoughts is not something you do once; it's something you do for the rest of your life. I have to decide every day which thoughts I will let grow. I have to choose every day whether to fight for my ideas or let them win. Every day, I have to keep growing and changing, stay committed no matter what I think, keep my emotions in check, and make room for learning and emotional growth that will last a lifetime.

It is true that thoughts that are not cared for can be dangerous. They can cause trauma, make people angry, and break up peace. But the power of thoughts that are challenged is stronger. They can mend wounds, bring back hope, and change lives. And so every day I choose to fight for my thoughts, to take them captive, to make them obey Christ, and to fill my mind with things that are true, good, right, pure, beautiful, and worthy of praise.

That is the way to be the best version of myself. That is the practice that keeps growth going, changes mistakes into lessons, balances emotions, and grows compassion. That is the discipline that keeps things from getting out of hand and making people angry. And that's the lesson I'll keep learning every day for the rest of my life.

Every day is a fight in your mind. Most people don't know how much they think, which is the truth. The danger isn't how many thoughts we have; it's how many we don't pay attention to. If you don't stop a thought, it can turn into a belief, and a belief can change your future.

Every day I choose to fight for my thoughts, to take them captive, to make them obey Christ, and to fill my mind with things that are true, good, right, pure, beautiful, and worthy of praise.

That is the way to be the best version of myself. That is the practice that keeps growth going, changes mistakes into lessons, balances emotions, and grows compassion. That is the kind of discipline that stops fights, anger, and rage. And that is the lesson I will keep learning for the rest of my life. Hope you can too!

VISION-DRIVEN
THINKING

I realize that vision-driven thinking doesn't come naturally to me when I think about it. Most of us live from day to day, reacting to what happens instead of planning how we want our lives to be. I know I did. I felt like I was just getting by some of the time—working hard, paying bills, and dealing with stress—but I knew deep down that God had more for me.

The Bible says in Proverbs 29:18, "*Where there is no vision, the people perish.*" That verse woke me up. I didn't want to go through life without a plan. I wanted to live with a purpose.

I remember a time when I was stuck in a job that made me feel bad. I hated going in every morning and came home tired every night. I was angry and doubted myself a lot. Jeremiah 29:11 spoke to me one day during my quiet time: "*For I know the plans I have for you... plans to give you hope and a future*."

I understood that if God had a plan for me, I had to make sure my thoughts were in line with that plan. I started to think, "*What kind of person do I want to be in ten years?*" "*What kind of life do I want to have?*" That change made everything different.

I stopped thinking about how bad things were right now and started thinking about how good they could be in the future. I imagined myself going to work with confidence, making a difference, and feeling good about what I had done when I left. I thought about how I would deal with difficult coworkers with patience instead of getting angry. Over time, those mental rehearsals started to change my life. Philippians 4:8 became my guide: "***Think about things that are true, noble, and right.***"

There was another time when money was tight. Bills were piling up, and fear told me I would never get ahead. My mind started to race with worry. But I remembered that being kind was part of my vision. I didn't want to be someone who was afraid of money; I wanted to be someone who trusted God and gave freely. Malachi 3:10 said to me, "***Bring the whole tithe into the storehouse...***" The Bible says, "***Test me in this.***"

I started to picture myself giving, even when it seemed impossible. I practiced how I would put my faith in God with my money. That vision gave me strength, and over time, I saw God give me things I never thought I would have.

Thinking based on my vision also affected how I dealt with stress. There was a time when I was worried about my health. The doctor's words made me feel shaky, and my mind raced with the worst things that could happen. Fear tried to take control. But I remembered Philippians 4:6–7: "***Do not worry about anything... and the peace of God... will guard your hearts and minds in Christ Jesus.***"

I started to picture myself walking in peace, even while I was waiting. I practiced how to breathe deeply, pray, and have faith in God no matter what happened. That mental practice didn't get rid of my fear completely, but it did give me a way to control my feelings instead of letting them control me.

Another story comes from a time when there was a lot of fighting between people. I was angry all the time because a friend broke my trust. I kept going over the pain again and again. But I knew that my goal was to be someone who forgives, not someone who holds on to anger. I started to picture myself letting go and going over in my head how I would respond with grace if I saw him again. Ephesians 4:32 said, "**Be kind and caring to each other, and forgive each other, just as God forgave you in Christ.**" That idea of forgiveness eventually came true.

Thinking based on your vision isn't just about big life goals; it's also about the choices you make every day. I remember mornings when I woke up feeling like I had already lost. My mind would start to think of all the things that could go wrong. I practiced visualization during those times. I imagined myself going through the day calmly, dealing with problems wisely, and ending the night with thanks. That mental practice gave me the strength to get through the day.

What I've learned is that thinking about the future requires self-control. This means writing down your goals, going over them every day, and making sure your thoughts match what the Bible says. In other words, it means asking yourself, "*Does this thought help me get closer to my vision or further away from it?*" It means deciding to think about things that are good and honourable, even when fear or anger tries to take over.

When I look back, I see that vision was not just about reaching my goals; it was also about becoming the person God wanted me to be. It was about standing up for my ideas and controlling my feelings so that my life was in line with His will. And I think other people can change in the same way.

Vision-driven thinking helps us move forward, whether we're dealing with a draining job, money problems, health issues, or relationship problems. It helps us get our thoughts in line with God's plan, see the future He has promised, and practice the kinds of responses that bring peace instead of chaos.

There was a time when I felt like I was going nowhere in my job. I would wake up with a knot in my stomach, scared of what the day would bring. I was so angry that I couldn't stop thinking about it: "*Why am I still here*?" Why hasn't anything changed? I remember sitting in my car before going into the office, holding the steering wheel, and praying, "*Lord, I don't want to live like this.*" That was a turning point. I understood that I would stay stuck if I kept letting my thoughts go to negative places. I needed to get my thoughts in line with what God wanted for my life. Jeremiah 29:11 made me remember that God had plans for me, plans to give me hope and a future.

I started to picture myself going to work with confidence, making a difference, and leaving with a sense of accomplishment. I practiced how I would deal with difficult coworkers by being patient instead of angry. Those mental rehearsals slowly started to change the way things were for me.

I have learned how important it is to write down your goals. I wrote down short-term goals, long-term goals and miracle goals for myself in journals. I wanted to get stronger in my faith, my character, and my ability to bounce back. I wanted to be a person of honour, who spoke kindly, and who walked in peace. Putting those goals down on paper made them real. Every morning, I went back to them and made my thoughts fit with that vision.

Meditating on Scripture became another tool. I memorized verses that fit with my vision and said them a lot. I said Isaiah 41:10: "***So do not fear, for I am with you***" when I was scared.

When I was feeling down, I repeated Galatians 6:9: *"**Let us not become weary in doing good, for at the proper time we will reap a harvest.**"* Those verses were like anchors that brought my mind back to God.

I used to think that vision-driven thinking was something reserved for pastors on Sunday mornings or motivational speakers with their flashy seminars. You know the type—big stages, bright lights, and promises that if you just dream big enough, the universe will conspire in I favour.

I remember sitting in my cramped apartment at 19 years old, all alone, where I started with pushing my vision of wanting to get married, travel the world with my wife and raise a God driven family. When my reality I wanted seems like a fantasy with bills on the table and a job that sucked the life out of me as a drywall taper, vision felt like a luxury I couldn't afford. It was a nice idea, sure, but how do you dream about a better tomorrow when today is kicking you in the teeth?

That all changed the day I truly let Proverbs 29:18 sink in: *"**Where there is no vision, the people perish.**"* The King James Version hits hard, doesn't it? Perish. Not just struggle or falter—perish. Like a plant wilting without water, a life without vision dries up and dies, even if the body keeps moving. I didn't want to perish. I was tired of perishing in slow motion.

Thirty-five years later, I see that dream that was formulated in my green kitchen table, became a reality. It has expanded with bonuses I never could have imagine. My job became my hobby, my marriage like a fairy tale and the children like a dream. Seven amazing children and awesome son-in-laws and a daughter-in-law all who are additional children to Kathleen and me. But let me take you back to one of the darkest seasons I've ever walked through. It was about fifteen years ago now, though it feels both like yesterday and a lifetime ago. My marriage was not in the place it is today. There was some trying times with work and family stress. It felt at times it was hanging on by a thread. Not the dramatic, explosive kind of hanging—more like the quiet erosion where you wake up one day and realize you're roommates who occasionally argue about whose turn it is to take out the trash. We had stopped dreaming together. Stopped praying together. Stopped even liking each other some days.

I wrote about the kind of husband I wanted to be in ten years. Not the guy who came home grumpy and scrolled on his phone while his wife handled everything. I wrote about a man who prayed with his wife every night, hugs and kisses were reciprocal, a man who led his family in devotions, who made his kids laugh so hard milk came out their noses. I wrote about a marriage where date nights weren't a distant memory but a non-negotiable rhythm. I wrote about vacations we'd take—not extravagant ones, but simple ones where we made memories that outlasted the credit card bill.

Then I wrote about our finances. Not just "get out of debt" (though that was definitely on there). I wrote about being the kind of people who gave ridiculously, who had margin to bless others, who never had to choose between groceries and medicine. I wrote about a house with a backyard big enough for the kids to run wild and a table long enough for neighbours to gather around.

I wrote about my relations with God. About being a man whose first thought in crisis wasn't panic but prayer. Whose default setting was faith, not fear.

When I was done, I had filled seven pages. My hand hurt. My eyes burned. But something in my chest felt… lighter. Like I'd just exhaled a breath I'd been holding for years.

And something began to shift.

It wasn't dramatic at first. More like the slow turning of a massive ship. But I started catching myself in moments where I would have reacted before—and choosing vision instead.

My physical health started changing. I had been carrying an extra fifty pounds for years, always too tired or stressed to do anything about it. But our vision included being healthy enough to play with our grandkids someday, to hike mountains as a family, to have energy for whatever God called us to. So I started small—just walking instead of driving when I could, choosing water over soda, doing push-ups while the coffee brewed. Nothing heroic. But vision made consistency possible where willpower never had.

The money stuff was the hardest. I won't pretend it wasn't. There were months where we literally didn't know how we were going to pay bills. But we had written down Malachi 3:10 as part of our vision— *"Bring the whole tithe into the storehouse... and see if I will not throw open the floodgates of heaven."* We decided that tithing wasn't about having extra—it was about honouring God first, no matter what.

One of the most powerful moments came about two years into this journey, when I went through my thoughts line by line. Am I the husband who prays with his wife every night? Check. Family devotions? Five days a week. Date nights? Almost every week, no matter what. vacations, multiple per year. Giving ridiculously? Not as much as I would like to. Working on a charity to support couples called Team2 – Two Shall become One", where two are better than one. House with a backyard? Sitting in it right now. We have a fire pit where the children enjoys. Healthy enough to play with grandkids? I'd just run a 5K that morning (slowly, but I finished). I started running 5-11K on a treadmill at the gym I attends almost five days a week.

I'm telling you this because I know what it's like to feel stuck. I know what it's like to wake up dreading the day, to feel like you're failing at everything that matters, to wonder if this is just how life is supposed to be.

God has more for you. Not just in heaven someday—right here, right now. But you have to choose it. You have to fight for it. You have to write it down and read it every day and let it change the way you think, one thought at a time.

Start small if you have to. One page. One sentence. "I am a person who…" and fill in the blank with whatever feels impossible right now. I am a person who walks in peace. I am a person who forgives quickly. I am a person who gives generously. I am a person who loves well.

Then tomorrow morning, before you check your phone, before you let the world tell you who you are, read it out loud. Let it be the first voice you hear.

Because where there is vision, people don't just survive. They come alive.

There's a story in the Bible that wrecks me every time I read it. It's about a guy named Joseph. You probably know it—sold into slavery by his own brothers, falsely accused and thrown into prison, forgotten for years. Most people would have given up. Most people would have become bitter and angry and stopped dreaming.

But Genesis 37:5 tells us something incredible: *"**Joseph had a dream, and when he told it to his brothers, they hated him all the more.**"*

That dream—God's vision for his life—sustained him through every dark season. When he was a slave, he served with excellence because he knew who he was becoming. When he was in prison, he interpreted dreams for others because he still believed in the God who gave dreams. When he stood before Pharaoh years later, he wasn't a broken man—he was a man who had been refined by vision.

And when his brothers finally stood before him, trembling because they knew what they'd done, Joseph didn't get revenge. He wept. Because the vision God gave him all those years ago wasn't just about position or power. It was about preservation. About saving his family. About God's bigger story.

That's what vision does. It doesn't just get you through the pit and the prison—it positions you for the palace. But more importantly, it transforms you in the process.

I think about the woman at the well in John 4. Jesus meets her in the middle of her mess—five failed marriages, living with a sixth guy, coming to draw water at noon because she's too ashamed to face the other women in the morning. Everyone in town has written her story for her: adulteress, failure, outcast.

But Jesus looks at her and basically says, "I see a different story. I see a woman who's going to tell this whole town about living water. I see the first evangelist in Samaria."

And because she dares to believe His vision for her life instead of the town's vision, she leaves her water jar, runs back to the very people who've rejected her, and says, "Come see a man who told me everything I ever did!" The Bible says many Samaritans believed because of her testimony.

That's the power of vision. It doesn't deny your past—it redeems it. It doesn't ignore your pain—it transforms it into purpose.

Vision didn't make those seasons painless. But it made them purposeful. Here's what I've learned: pain without vision creates victims. Pain with vision creates victors.

When you know where you're going, the hard things become stepping stones instead of stumbling blocks. The dark seasons become chapters instead of the whole story.

I love how Habakkuk 2:2-3 puts it: *"**Write down the revelation and make it plain on tablets so that a herald may run with it. For the revelation awaits an appointed time; it speaks of the end and will not prove false. Though it linger, wait for it; it will certainly come and will not delay**."*

Write it down. Make it plain. So that whoever reads it may run. That's what I did. I wrote it down. I made it plain. And now I'm running.

Not perfectly. I still fight. I still fail. I still have mornings where I wake up anxious and have to choose vision all over again. But I am running.

I've learned something profound: the limitation isn't God's power—it's our imagination. That's why vision matters so much. Because when we dare to dream with God, when we write down the wild things He whispers to our hearts in the quiet, we create space for the immeasurably more.

We give God a canvas to paint on. We give the Holy Spirit room to move. We give faith legs to run.

So here's my challenge to you today, right now, wherever you're reading this:

Get a piece of paper. Or open the notes app on your phone. Or grab that journal that's been collecting dust. And start writing your vision. Not what you think is possible. Not what your bank account says is realistic. Not what your critics or your past or your fears say you deserve.

Write what God says.

Write who He says you are.

Write where He wants to take you.

Write the marriage you want.

The parenting you long for.

The character you're becoming.

The impact you'll make.

The freedom you'll walk in.

The joy that will mark your days.

Write it in present tense, like it's already true. Because in God's economy, it is.

I am…

We are…

Our family will be…

By God's grace, I will become…

Then tomorrow morning, read it out loud.

And the next day.

And the day after that.

Until the person you're becoming starts showing up in the person you are today. Until your thoughts start lining up with God's thoughts. Until your reactions start looking like Jesus. Until your life starts telling a different story. Because where there is no vision, the people perish. But where there is vision—clear, written, spoken, fought-for vision?

That's where people come alive. That's where marriages are restored. That's where addictions are broken. That's where children rise up and call their parents blessed. That's where ordinary becomes extraordinary. That's where perishing turns into flourishing. Friend, your vision is waiting. Not in some far-off someday. Right now. Today.

Will you write it?

Will you read it?

Will you live it?

Someone is waiting on the other side of your obedience. Your future spouse. Your future children. Your future ministry. Your future self. And most importantly, your Father in heaven who's been dreaming over you since before you were born.

He's not done with you. He's just getting started. So write the vision. Make it plain. And watch God do immeasurably more. The best is yet to come. I promise.

FEED and FUEL *Your*
BRAIN

The brain is a natural wonder because it has billions of neurons that work together in a very complicated way. It controls how we think, feel, remember things, and do things. The brain, like any other part of our body, needs the right nutrients to work well. It needs just the right amounts of nutrients, vitamins, minerals, and water to do its complicated jobs well.

Five years ago I stood frozen in the pulpit, staring at two hundred people while my mind went completely blank. I had forgotten the third point of my own sermon. That night I wept in the shower and begged God not to let my mind slip away while I still had so much Kingdom work to do. A week later my doctor handed me bloodwork that felt like a divine wake-up call: B12 almost undetectable, omega-3 index in the bottom 5%, chronic dehydration, creeping blood sugar.

In that moment 1 Corinthians 6:19–20 hit me like never before: *"**Do you not know that your body is a temple of the Holy Spirit within you, whom you have from God? You are not your own, for you were bought with a price. So glorify God in your body**."*

In "Feeding and Fuelling the Brain," we will go on an enlightening journey to learn about how nutrition is important for brain health. We will talk about how eating foods that are good for your brain can make you smarter and how getting the right amount of macronutrients can help your brain work at its best.

There is a very interesting part of the gut-brain connection that goes beyond what we usually think of as food. The intricate interplay between the gut microbiome and the brain has garnered significant attention, highlighting the direct impact of digestive health on mental wellness (Williams et al., 2023).

For months I woke up at 3 a.m. with my heart racing and my thoughts spiraling. I would pray, quote Scripture, put on worship music—sometimes it helped, most nights it didn't. Then I started eating fermented foods every single day: sauerkraut on eggs, kefir in smoothies, homemade kimchi with dinner. Three weeks later the panic attacks vanished. Science calls it the gut-brain axis; I experienced Philippians 4:7 in real time—*"**the peace of God, which surpasses all comprehension, will guard your hearts and your minds in Christ Jesus**."*

We also often forget how important it is to stay hydrated. Learning how to stay hydrated can have a big impact on how well our brains work and how well we think. This can help us think more clearly and stay focused.

I used to live on coffee and soda. By 2 p.m. I was foggy, irritable, and useless. I forced myself to drink 100–120 ounces of water a day. Four days later the brain fog lifted like someone had opened the windows in my skull. Jesus offered living water (John 4:14) and still asked for a drink on the cross (John 19:28). If the Son of God honoured the body's need for hydration, I decided I would too.

You can't talk about brain health without mentioning vitamins, minerals, and antioxidants. Some nutrients are very important for how our brains work. We can make better food choices that are good for our brain health by learning how these micronutrients affect the brain (Smith & Johnson, 2022).

We need to pay full attention to sleep, which is another important part of keeping our brains healthy. We need to stress how important restorative sleep is and how it has a big effect on how our brains work. We can learn how sleep helps us remember things, keep our emotions in check, and be mentally strong overall by learning more about it.

I used to brag that I only needed five hours of sleep. Then Psalm 127:2 wrecked me: *"**It is in vain that you rise up early and go late to rest, eating the bread of anxious toil; for he gives to his beloved sleep.**"*

I started protecting a 11 p.m. to 7 a.m. window like it was sacred. The first week I felt guilty for "wasting time." By week two I was waking up before my alarm with sermon ideas flooding my mind. Sleep is when God literally washes toxins out of your brain.

We also need to look into nootropics and supplements that improve brain function to learn more about how what we eat and drink can change the way our brains work.

I'm cautious—God gave us food as medicine first (Genesis 1:29). But when bloodwork confirmed deficiencies, my doctor prescribed therapeutic doses of fish oil, methyl-B12, vitamin D3, and magnesium glycinate. The difference was undeniable and felt like a gift straight from the Lord's hand.

The choices we make can make our brains healthier and help us think better. We can get the most out of our brains by understanding how nutrition, hydration, sleep, and brain function are all related.

Eating healthy is very important for keeping your brain healthy and your mind sharp (Smith & Johnson, 2022). The brain needs a lot of energy and nutrients all the time to work well. The brain needs the right building blocks and fuel to do its complicated work, and the food we eat gives it those things.

Antioxidants protect the brain from oxidative stress and free radicals (Jones et al., 2020).

Antioxidants are things like vitamins C and E, beta-carotene, and flavonoids that are found in colourful fruits and vegetables like berries, citrus fruits, spinach, kale, and broccoli.

Every morning I blend two handfuls of frozen berries with spinach and kefir. My wife call it "Harrison's purple potion." It's Daniel 1:12–15 in a blender.

Choline is a necessary nutrient for the growth of the brain, learning, and memory (Davis et al., 2018). It is a precursor to acetylcholine, a neurotransmitter that helps the brain work better. Foods that are high in choline include eggs, liver, soybeans, fish, and cruciferous vegetables.

I try to eat three or four pastured eggs almost every day now. A lot of fruits, vegetables, whole grains, fish, olive oil, and a little bit of red wine are all part of the Mediterranean diet. This diet has been linked to a lower risk of cognitive decline and neurodegenerative diseases (Johnson et al., 2019). This way of eating gives you a lot of nutrients and antioxidants that are good for your brain and may help keep your mind sharp as you get older.

Chronic inflammation can damage brain health and lead to cognitive decline (Adams et al., 2021). Inflammation can get worse if you eat a lot of processed foods, refined sugars, and unhealthy fats and not enough foods that are high in nutrients. An anti-inflammatory diet rich in fruits, vegetables, whole grains, healthy fats (including olive oil, avocados, and nuts), and lean proteins can reduce inflammation and enhance cerebral health.

When I cut refined sugar and seed oils for forty days as a fast unto the Lord, my chronic joint pain vanished, my skin cleared, and most amazingly, my prayer life became electric. Inflammation had been muffling my ability to hear God's voice.

Recent research has emphasized the importance of the gut-brain axis, the bidirectional communication network connecting the gut and the brain (Williams et al., 2023). The gut microbiota, which is made up of trillions of bacteria that live in our digestive system, is a very important part of this communication. Eating a variety of foods that are high in fiber can help keep your gut microbiota healthy.   This   can help your brain work better and make you feel better mentally.

To keep your brain healthy and improve your thinking skills for the rest of your life, you need to eat a balanced diet that is high in nutrients and includes foods that are good for your brain (Smith & Johnson, 2022). A healthy diet, regular exercise, enough sleep, and mental stimulation are all important for a healthy brain.

Eating a balanced diet that includes brain-healthy foods can have a big impact on how well our brains work and how healthy they are overall. Omega-3 fatty acids are very important for the health and growth of the brain. They have been linked to better brain function and a lower risk of cognitive decline as you get older (Jernerén et al., 2020). Salmon, mackerel, and sardines are all fatty fish that are high in omega-3s. We can get protein from plants like flaxseeds, chia seeds, and walnuts if we don't eat meat or dairy.

Blueberries, strawberries, and blackberries are all berries that are high in antioxidants and other things that have been shown to help the brain work better. They help lower oxidative stress and inflammation, which are both linked to cognitive decline that happens as we age.

Dark chocolate with a lot of cocoa (70% or more) has flavonoids in it. These are antioxidants and anti-inflammatories. These substances can help blood flow to the brain and improve its function. You should only eat a little bit of dark chocolate because it has a lot of calories and sugar.

Kale, spinach, and broccoli are all leafy greens that are good for your brain because they are full of vitamins and minerals. Lutein, folate, beta-carotene, and vitamin K are just a few of the vitamins, minerals, and antioxidants they contain. Researchers have found that these nutrients can help the brain work better and lower the risk of dementia.

Turmeric is a spice that is often used in Indian food. It contains curcumin, which is a chemical. Curcumin is a powerful antioxidant and anti-inflammatory that may help memory and lower the risk of diseases that cause the brain to break down.

Brown rice, quinoa, oats, and whole wheat bread are all whole grains that give the brain a steady supply of glucose, which is its main source of energy. They also have fiber, which helps keep your blood sugar levels steady and gives you energy all day.

Almonds, walnuts, pumpkin seeds, and sunflower seeds are all nuts and seeds that are good for your brain because they are full of healthy fats, vitamin E, antioxidants, and other nutrients. Some people say that these foods can help you remember things and think.

Don't forget that foods that are good for your brain should be part of a healthy diet. You need to eat a lot of different foods in moderation to get a lot of brain-healthy nutrients. Also, it's a good idea to talk to a doctor or registered dietitian about your health and dietary needs.

It is important to balance macronutrients, which are the nutrients that the body needs in large amounts, for brain health and the best cognitive function. The three main macronutrients are fats, proteins, and carbohydrates. All of these macronutrients are very important for keeping your brain healthy, giving you energy, and keeping neurotransmitters working.

Carbohydrates give the brain most of its energy. Your body turns carbs into glucose when you eat them. Brain cells use glucose as energy. Examples of complex carbohydrates that slowly release glucose over time are whole grains, fruits, and vegetables. This keeps your energy levels stable and your brain working. Refined sugars can make you crash and hurt your brain, so it's best to avoid them and choose healthy, whole carbs instead.

Proteins are needed to make neurotransmitters, which are the chemicals that let brain cells talk to each other. Dopamine, serotonin, and norepinephrine are all neurotransmitters that play a big role in mood, focus, and memory. Eating lean meats, fish, eggs, dairy products, legumes, and nuts, which are all good sources of protein, can help your body make the amino acids it needs to make neurotransmitters.

Healthy fats are good for the brain because they make up a lot of the brain's structure and help protect and insulate nerve cells (Jernerén et al., 2020).

We need to eat the right amounts of these macronutrients to keep our brains working well. It's important to keep in mind that everyone's dietary needs are different. This is because of things like their age, how active they are, and their overall health. You can talk to a doctor or a registered dietitian to make sure you're getting the right amount of macronutrients for your brain health.

You should pay attention to more than just macronutrients. Vitamins and minerals are examples of micronutrients that are also very important for brain function. Getting enough of important vitamins and minerals, like vitamin B12, folate, vitamin D, magnesium, and zinc, is important for your brain to work well (Smith et al., 2021).

B vitamins, like B1 (thiamine), B6 (pyridoxine), B9 (folate), and B12 (cobalamin), help make neurotransmitters like serotonin, dopamine, and norepinephrine. They help brain cells get energy. Not getting enough of these vitamins can make it hard to think, feel good, and stay calm (Begum & Richardson, 2020).

Vitamin C is a powerful antioxidant that shields the brain from oxidative stress (Harrison et al., 2022).

Vitamin E is another powerful antioxidant that keeps the membranes of brain cells from being damaged by oxidation (Ames et al., 2021).

Magnesium is involved in more than 300 chemical reactions in the body, some of which are important for how the brain works (Guerrera et al., 2018).

Zinc is important for the brain to grow and work right (Rahman et al., 2021).

It's important to remember that these vitamins and minerals are good for your brain, but you should get them from food instead of just supplements. Your brain needs a lot of different nutrients to work well. Eating a lot of different foods, like fruits, vegetables, whole grains, lean proteins, and healthy fats, can help.

It's very important for your brain to get enough good sleep. You might want to skip sleep to get more done, but you should know how sleep affects your health and how well your brain works.

While you sleep, your brain does things that are important for it to work right. One of these processes is putting memories together. Getting enough sleep helps us remember and use new information better.

Also, sleep is very important for keeping your feelings in check. When we prioritize sleep, we allow our brains to return to a healthy emotional state.

Getting enough sleep is also very important for keeping your brain working well all day. A good night's sleep helps us wake up feeling refreshed and alert.

Also, not getting enough sleep has been linked to a higher risk of getting neurological diseases like Alzheimer's disease and other types of dementia.

A lot of people take nootropics and brain-boosting supplements to make their brains work better and think more clearly. Before taking certain supplements and nootropics, you should talk to a doctor and be careful. But if you use these substances the right way, they can be good for your brain health.

We can improve our brain health by paying attention to what we eat, how much water we drink, how much sleep we get, and how we live our lives. This chapter teaches us how to make smart choices and put our mental health first. We can work toward better mental clarity, better cognitive performance, and a healthy brain for the rest of our lives by being careful about what we eat and how we fuel our brains.

What started as a desperate attempt to save my mind has become daily worship. Every egg, every handful of berries, every glass of water, every early bedtime is now an offering: *"Lord, here is my brain—use it for Your glory."* And He is. The fog is gone. The fear is gone. The joy is back. And I've never felt more alive in my calling.

REWRITE *your inner*
NARATIVE

I wake up every day with a story already in my head. At times, it is a tale of faith, hope, and bravery. At other times, it is a story of fear, doubt, and insecurity. Over the years, I've learned that the story I choose to tell myself affects not only how I feel but also what I do, how I relate to others, and my future. The Bible says, "***For as he thinketh in his heart, so is he***" (Proverbs 23:7). The thoughts we cultivate give rise to our reality. If I let negative thoughts take over, I am living in defeat. But when I use God's truth to change the story in my head, I win.

There was a time in my life when I kept telling myself, "*I'm not good enough.*" Every problem made me feel like I wasn't good enough. But over time, with prayer, scripture, and deliberate practice, I started to change that story. I began to say to myself, "***I am fearfully and wonderfully made***" (Psalm 139:14). That one change started to change my confidence, my relationships, and even my job. It became a daily habit for me to rewrite my inner story instead of just once.

Weeds in the mind's garden are like negative thoughts. If not stopped, they spread quickly and take away joy and peace. I had to learn how to reframe things, which is just pulling out the weeds and planting seeds of truth instead. The first thing to do was to be aware. I had to stop and pay attention when my thoughts were going crazy. When I made a mistake at work, my old story would say, "*You always fail.*" But now I stop that thought before it grows. The Bible says, "*We destroy arguments and every false claim that goes against the knowledge of God, and we take every thought captive to make it obey Christ*" (2 Corinthians 10:5).

When I catch the thought, I put it to the test. I wonder if this is true. Does this agree with what God says? Most of the time, the answer is no. The enemy lives on lies, but God's Word is the truth. For example, when I feel bad about myself, I think of Romans 8:1: "*There is now no condemnation for those who are in Christ Jesus.*"

I change my mind. Instead of saying, "*I'm a failure,*" I say, "*Through Him who loved me, I am more than a conqueror*" (Romans 8:37). This three-step process—catch, challenge, change—has saved my life.

Words are powerful. How I talk to myself affects how I act in the world. I used to wake up and think right away, "This day is going to be hard." But now, I start on purpose with affirmations based on the Bible. I tell myself, "*This is the day the Lord has made; I will be happy and rejoice in it*" (Psalm 118:24).

I say softly, "*I can do all things through Christ who strengthens me*" (Philippians 4:13).

One personal story that stands out is when I was getting ready for a big presentation and was very nervous. I kept hearing my inner voice say, "*You're going to mess this up.*" I stopped, prayed, and started saying good things about myself: "**God has not given me a spirit of fear, but of power, love, and a sound mind**" (2 Timothy 1:7).

That change in how I talked to myself gave me the strength to stand up straight and do what I needed to do. When you talk to yourself in a way that gives you power, you're not ignoring reality; you're choosing to see it through the eyes of faith.

It's a gift to be clear in a world full of noise. Focus is the skill of directing our mental energy toward what is important. For years, I had a hard time staying focused. My phone, social media, and notifications kept me from doing what God wanted me to do. But discipline is like training your mind, just like athletes train their bodies. Paul says, "**Do you not know that all the runners in a race run, but only one wins the prize?**" Run in a way that will win you the prize. It is written in 1 Corinthians 9:24–25 that "*everyone who competes in the games goes into strict training.*"

For me, mental discipline means making time each morning for prayer and reading the Bible before I check my phone, breaking tasks into short, focused blocks of time, and saying "*no*" to things that don't help me reach my goals.

I sat down to write one morning, but I kept getting distracted by emails. I stopped and prayed, reminding myself of Psalm 46:10: "**Be still, and know that I am God.**" That stillness helped me see things more clearly, and I finished the work with peace.

Attention is like a light that shines on you. That area gets bigger wherever I shine it. But things that get in the way scatter the light and make me tired. Jesus was a great example of how to pay attention. "**Jesus often went to lonely places to pray,**" says Luke 5:16. He got rid of anything that might have kept him from being with the Father. I started doing this by making sacred spaces in my day, like turning off notifications while I pray, setting aside time to think, and choosing meaningful conversations over mindless scrolling.

I was thinking about work emails while having dinner with my family one night. I realized I hadn't heard my daughter when she asked me a question. That moment made me feel guilty. Since then, I always put my phone away when I'm with my family. Love is paying attention.

You don't just get mentally sharp; you have to work at it every day. One of my anchors is the Bible: "*Your word is a lamp to my feet and a light to my path*" (Psalm 119:105).

Another option is to keep a gratitude journal. I write down three things I'm thankful for every day. Even when life is hard, I can find things to be thankful for, like the sunrise, a kind word, or the breath in my lungs. Being thankful changes how I see things and makes me more aware of God's goodness.

Exercise makes my body stronger and clears my mind. Rest is just as important. Taking a break and letting my mind rest has given me more energy and clarity.

One of my favourite things to do is to be thankful when I wake up. I write down my blessings even when things are tough. That practice helps me remember that God's mercies are new every day. It helps me think better when I see chances instead of problems. These daily habits have made me stronger over time. They have helped me focus better, see things more clearly, and believe more strongly.

It has taken faith, discipline, and daily practice to rewrite my inner story. It's not about being perfect; it's about making progress. Every time I notice a bad thought, speak the truth, focus my mind, and sharpen my mind, I get closer to the person God made me to be. Romans 12:2 says, "*Don't follow the pattern of this world; instead, let your mind be renewed.*" That renewal is still going on. Every day, we choose to rewrite the story with God's truth.

LIVING as your HIGHEST SELF

When I got off the plane in Canada in 1988, I was only 18 years old. I was both excited and scared at the same time. I had left behind everything I knew and that made me feel safe, and I was going into a land that felt big, cold, and strange. I didn't have any family or friends here to help me out, and I didn't have a safety net to catch me if I fell. I only had a strong feeling inside me that Canada was meant to be my home. I also believed that if I stood up for my beliefs and learned to control my feelings, I could handle anything that came my way.

The first year was very hard. I worked on a tobacco farm and lived in a bunkhouse that didn't keep the cold out very well. The air was so sharp at 4:30 a.m. that it felt like knives against my skin. I was already in the fields by 5 a.m., and my hands were sore from the cold and my body was sore from bending over rows of tobacco plants. The pay was $5.25 an hour, which was something, but not enough to live on. I remember lying in bed at night, my muscles hurting, my stomach growling, and my mind telling me to give up. But I said no. I told myself that this wasn't the end of my story. This was the start.

Being able to talk about my thoughts saved my life. I learned quickly that if I let despair take hold, it would take over my life. So I bravely talked to myself. I told myself that the cold would go away, that the pain was making me stronger, and that being alone was teaching me to trust God. I wouldn't cry wolf or ask for sympathy from others because I knew that if I gave in to self-pity, I would weaken the spirit that needed to grow stronger.

I didn't live in a home; I lived in a barn. Winters were very harsh. The gas in the well often ran out, so I had no heat. The driveway was over 500 feet long and covered in four or five feet of snow. The water froze. I remember nights when I wrapped myself in every blanket I could find and shivered until morning, asking God for strength. My mother came to see me that first year, and when she saw how things were, she cried. I couldn't let her tears break my will, even though they broke my heart. I said to her, "*This is where I belong*." "Canada is my home." I saw fate, but she only saw hardship.

There were times when people used me. I put in a lot of effort, but I didn't always get what I deserved. I was young, inexperienced, and weak, and some people thought I would be easy to take advantage of. But even then, I wouldn't let anger take over. I told myself that God, not other people, defined my worth. I kept going, sure that the right doors would open if I stayed true to myself.

And then, one day, I ran into Cor Visser at the church I attend. He had a drywall business, and he saw something in me that other people didn't. He stood up for me, gave me chances, and was a big part of helping me get my immigration papers. Cor was more than just a boss; he was a mentor, a guide, and a reminder that God puts the right people in our lives at the right time. His presence showed me that I was not alone and that God was planting seeds of hope even in the coldest winters.

I now see that those years were not just about staying alive; they were also about changing. Even when fear told me I would fail, I learned to act confident. Even when storms raged around me, I learned how to stay calm. I learned to stay focused on my goals, even when the future looked uncertain. I became a thought leader in my own life by not letting other people define me or my circumstances decide my future.

There were a lot of stories of people along the way that helped me get through tough times. I remember one winter when the snow was so deep that I could hardly get down the driveway. I didn't have enough money for good boots, so I wrapped my feet in plastic bags and socks and walked through the snow with determination. It hurt to walk, but I kept telling myself, "*This won't last forever.*" "*This is making me who I am.*" And it did. That winter taught me how to be strong and how to keep going even when the road is blocked.

I was working long hours and barely making enough to eat at another time. I remember sitting in the barn, tired and hungry, and wanting to give up. Instead, I opened my Bible and read words that made me think of how faithful God is. I prayed, and at that moment, I felt at peace. The hunger and tiredness didn't go away, but my spirit did. I learned then that living as your best self doesn't mean avoiding hard times; it means finding strength in the middle of them.

There were also times when people were nice to me that made me feel less alone. I remember a neighbour who brought me food during a very cold winter. It was a small thing, but it meant a lot to me. It made me remember that God puts the right people in your life at the right time, and that you are always seen, even when you feel like you are not.

I learned that living as your best self means never giving up. It means standing up for your ideas, controlling your feelings, and trusting

God's plan. It's about having faith that every problem is a lesson, every challenge is a chance to grow, and every moment is part of a bigger plan.

When I think back to that eighteen-year-old boy in the tobacco fields, in the barn, and in the cold winters, I smile. He didn't quit. He didn't give up. He lived as his best self, even when life gave him every reason to give up. And that's the lesson I take with me: you can always be your best self, no matter where you are or what you're going through. People who are brave choose to have confidence, peace, and purpose, not people who are lucky.

I often think about those nights in the barn when the cold was all around me and the only sound was the silence. During those times, I learned what faith really meant. I had no one to help me or comfort me, but I did have the Word of God. When the cold was too much to bear, I would whisper to myself the words of Psalm 23:4: "*Even though I walk through the valley of the shadow of death, I will fear no evil, for you are with me; your rod and your staff, they comfort me.*" Those words became my blanket, my food, and my strength when I was too tired to go on.

Some days I wondered why life had to be so hard. Why did I have to get up at 4:30 a.m.? to work in fields that are freezing for $5.25 an hour? Why did I have to live in a barn with no heat, no running water, and no comfort? But then I remembered Romans 5:3 4: "*Not only that, but we rejoice in our sufferings, knowing that suffering produces endurance, and endurance produces character, and character produces hope.*" My suffering had a purpose. It was making people stronger. It was making me who I am. It was giving me hope deep down.

I learned that living as my best self isn't about avoiding hard times; it's about trusting God in the middle of them. It means being confident when fear whispers, bringing peace when storms rage, and having a purpose when the road ahead looks unclear. You need to be the thought leader in your own life. You need to stand up for your ideas, control your feelings, and not let distractions get in the way of your destiny.

I remember one night when the cold was so bad that I felt completely alone. I cried out to God and asked Him why I had to go through so much pain. I felt His presence at that moment. I remembered Jeremiah 29:11: "*For I know the plans I have for you, declares the Lord, plans for welfare and not for evil, to give you a future and a hope.*" Those words reminded me that my pain was not the end; it was a way to get ready for the future God had planned for me.

I started to see the results of my hard work at some point. The years of hardship were not wasted; they were seeds planted in my spirit. Every cold night in the barn, every long day as a drywall taper, working in the tobacco fields, mushroom barn, and every moment of loneliness had made me into someone who could stand tall and be confident, peaceful, and purposeful.

I remember a time when the drywall taping slow down slowed down and I didn't have much money to live on. I was tempted to give up, but I remembered Matthew 6:33: "*But seek first the kingdom of God and his righteousness, and all these things will be added to you.*" I chose to believe that God would provide, even when I had no money. And He did. There were chances that started to open up, small at first, but enough to keep me going.

Another story when I was discriminated against. There were times when people looked down on me, ignored me, or tried to take advantage of me because I was young, brown skin guy, foreign, and new to the country. It hurt, but I remembered 1 Peter 2:9: "*But you are a chosen race, a royal priesthood, a holy nation, a people for his own possession, that you may proclaim the excellencies of him who called you out of darkness into his marvelous light.*" Those words reminded me that God, not other people, defined who I was. I was picked, I was called, and I belonged to Him. And that helped me get over the bad things.

There were times when I felt very lonely. I wanted to be with someone who could help me carry the load. Instead of giving up hope, I read Psalm 34:18: "***The Lord is near to the broken-hearted and saves the crushed in spirit.***" This made me realize that I wasn't alone, even though I felt alone. God was close, closer than I could have imagined, and His presence was all I needed to get through.

This is when God brought Kathleen into my life and she has from then till now kept me warm and is always by my side. My equal half. Ecclesiastes 4:9 10: "***Two are better than one, because they have a good reward for their work.***"

Over time, I started to see the big picture. Living as your best self doesn't mean avoiding hard times; it means accepting them as a way to get ready. It's about standing up for your ideas, controlling your feelings, and believing in God's plan. It's about being the boss of your own life, not letting fear, doubt, or distraction control you, and instead leading yourself with courage, wisdom, and faith.

I started to exude confidence over time—not arrogance, but the quiet knowledge that I could get through it. I carried peace with me, which was not the absence of struggle but the calm in the storm. I had a purpose that was like a compass that led me through every season, not a destination. I took charge of my own thoughts and refused to let other people or situations decide my future.

To live as your best self, you need to believe that God has a job for you. It means believing that every challenge is a chance to grow, every trial is a chance to learn, and every moment is part of a bigger plan. It means remembering what Romans 8:28 says: "***And we know that for those who love God all things work together for good, for those who are called according to his purpose.***"

I smile when I think about that eighteen-year-old boy who worked in the tobacco fields and the barn during the cold winters. He didn't give up. He lived as his best self, even when life gave him every reason to give up. And that's the lesson I take with me: you can be your best self no matter where you are or what you're going through. Stand up for your ideas. Control your feelings. Trust what God has planned for you.

"And let us not grow weary of doing good, for in due season we will reap, if we do not give up," is something I think about a lot. Those words are the heart of my story. I didn't give up, and in the end, I got what I wanted. Not just money stability or immigration papers, but the deeper reward of knowing that I had lived faithfully, bravely, and with a purpose.

So, I tell anyone who hears my story to live as their best self. Don't let hard times define you. Don't let things that aren't important get in the way. Don't let fear stop you from speaking. Stand up for your ideas. Control your feelings. Put your faith in God's plan. And don't forget that faith, peace, and purpose are not things that only the lucky get. They are choices made by the brave, kept up by faith, and rewarded by God.

Most of us spend our days living as a fraction of who God created us to be. We wake up tired, scroll through other people's highlight reels, drag ourselves to jobs that drain us, come home numb, and collapse into bed promising tomorrow will be different. Then tomorrow comes and we do it all again. I know because I lived that way for years. I preached about abundant life on Sundays while secretly wondering if this exhausted, anxious, overweight, short-tempered version of me was all there was.

Then one morning everything cracked open. I was reading Romans 12:1–2 and the words leapt off the page like they were written in fire:

"Therefore, I urge you, brothers and sisters, in view of God's mercy, to offer your bodies as a living sacrifice, holy and pleasing to

God—this is your true and proper worship. Do not conform to the pattern of this world, but be transformed by the renewing of your mind. Then you will be able to test and approve what God's will is— his good, pleasing and perfect will."

I had read those verses hundreds of times, but that day the Holy Spirit whispered, "*You are not offering Me your highest self. You are offering Me the leftovers.*" I closed my Bible, walked to the mirror, and looked at the man staring back: thirty-nine years old, forty pounds overweight, chronically tired, medicating stress with food and Netflix, preaching transformation while refusing to be transformed. I started crying because I realized I had been conforming to the pattern of this world and calling it "normal ministry life."

Living as your highest self is not a luxury for the spiritually elite. It is obedience. It is the only reasonable response to the mercy of Jesus who gave everything so we could have everything (John 10:10). It is what Paul meant when he wrote, "***I have been crucified with Christ and I no longer live, but Christ lives in me***" (Galatians 2:20). The highest version of you is not you trying harder. It is Christ fully alive in you.

That morning I made a decision: I will stop bringing God the scraps of my energy, the dregs of my focus, and the wreckage of my health and start bringing Him the first fruits of my body, mind, and time. That decision changed everything.

The first thing I had to face was the lie that "*highest self*" living is selfish. I had bought the Christian version of hustle culture that says rest is laziness, boundaries are unloving, and taking care of your body is vanity. Jesus destroyed that lie when He withdrew to lonely places to pray (Luke 5:16), when He slept in a storm (Mark 4:38), when He turned water into wine so a party could keep going (John 2:1–11). The same Jesus who said "***love your neighbor as yourself***" (Mark 12:31) assumed we would love ourselves enough to steward the one body, one mind, and one life He gave us.

I started small but radical. I cleared my calendar for thirty days and asked one question every time something was requested of me: *"Is this the highest and best use of the life Jesus died to give me?"* I said no to good things so I could say yes to God things. I turned off notifications. I started going to bed at 10 p.m. I started walking every morning while listening to Scripture instead of news. I ate food that made me feel alive instead of food that made me feel guilty. I scheduled weekly sabbaths where my phone stayed in a drawer and my family got the unhurried version of me.

People thought I was having a midlife crisis. My colleagues asked if I was depressed. My wife was not sure what was going on. But something wild happened: the more I honoured God with my body and time, the more of Him I experienced. Joy came back. Creativity exploded. I started hearing God's voice again—not just for sermons but for my actual life. I lost thirty-five pounds in six months without trying. My marriage went from surviving to thriving. My kids started saying, "Dad, you're fun again."

Living as your highest self is not about becoming impressive. It is about becoming available. Available to God. Available to the people you love. Available to the dreams He planted in you before you were born (Jeremiah 1:5).

Ephesians 2:10 says we are God's handiwork, created in Christ Jesus to do good works which He prepared in advance for us to do. The Greek word for handiwork is poiēma—the same word we get "poem" from. You are God's poetry. But when we live tired, distracted, and unhealthy, we are God's poetry with coffee stains and crumpled pages. Living as your highest self is simply letting the Author present His masterpiece unmarred.

I love how The Message translates Romans 12:1–2: ***"Take your everyday, ordinary life—your sleeping, eating, going-to-work, and*** *walking-around life—and place it before God as an offering*." That is highest-self living: every ordinary moment offered holy.

Here is what I have learned in the years since that mirror moment:

First, your highest self wakes up with God, not to the world. "*Very early in the morning, while it was still dark, Jesus got up, left the house and went off to a solitary place, where he prayed*" (Mark 1:35). I started setting my alarm thirty minutes earlier than necessary just to sit with Jesus before the demands started. Those thirty minutes saved my life.

Second, your highest self moves. "*Bodily exercise profits a little*" (1 Timothy 4:8, KJV) is often quoted to minimize exercise, but Paul was saying it profits—period. I started lifting weights three to five days a week and walking. My body is stronger at fifty-seven than it was at thirty-four, and my mind is sharper because of it.

Third, your highest self eats to live, not lives to eat. I stopped treating my body like a dumpster for stress and started treating meals like communion with the God who provides. "*Whether you eat or drink... do it all for the glory of God*" (1 Corinthians 10:31).

Fourth, your highest self says no so you can say yes. Jesus often withdrew from crowds who wanted more of Him to be with the Father (Luke 5:16). Boundaries are not unchristlike. They are Christlike.

Fifth, your highest self forgives quickly and loves fiercely because tomorrow is not promised. "*Do not let the sun go down while you are still angry*" (Ephesians 4:26). I stopped carrying yesterday's offenses into today's opportunities.

Sixth, your highest self remembers you are dust and treats yourself with compassion. "*He remembers that we are dust*" (Psalm 103:14). I stopped shaming myself for being human and started thanking God for grace that is new every morning.

Last, your highest self lives from approval, not for approval. *"Am I now trying to win the approval of human beings, or of God?"* (Galatians 1:10). When you know you are beloved, you stop performing and start becoming.

I wish I could tell you this way of living is easy. It is not. The world will call you selfish. Religious people will call you worldly. Your flesh will scream for the old familiar numbness. But Jesus called it abundant life, and He never lied.

Today I am stronger, healthier, happier, and more on fire for Jesus than I have ever been. I preach better. I love better. I lead better. I live better. Not because I am special, but because I finally stopped sabotaging the masterpiece God made.

You are not stuck with the tired, overwhelmed, barely-getting-by version of you. That is not God's best. That is the world's pattern. The highest version of you is waiting on the other side of daily decisions to honour the temple, the time, and the talents Jesus died to redeem.

"His divine power has given us everything we need for a godly life through our knowledge of him who called us by his own glory and goodness" (2 Peter 1:3).

Everything you need is already yours in Christ. Now live like it.

CONCLUSION

You made it.

You began this journey in a hospital parking lot with me, rain pounding the roof while panic pounded my chest, and now here we are on the other side. The storm in your mind may not have completely stopped, but you are no longer drowning in it. You are standing in the boat, feet planted, eyes fixed on Jesus, speaking peace to the waves you once thought would swallow you whole.

Look at what you now carry that you did not have when you opened the first page.

You know how to champion your thoughts instead of letting them champion you. You have learned to take every single one captive to the obedience of Christ, because you finally believe that your mind belongs to Jesus and was never meant to be a playground for the enemy.

You have challenged your thoughts with the fierce tenderness of a lawyer who refuses to let lies testify unchallenged. Philippians 4:8 is no longer a nice suggestion hanging on a coffee mug; it is the filter through which every thought must now pass or be evicted.

You have mastered your emotions, not by denying them, not by stuffing them, but by inviting Jesus into the middle of them. You have discovered that feelings are data, not directives, and that you can feel deeply without sinning wildly.

You have laid down the victim card forever. You may have been wounded, betrayed, abandoned, and abused, but you are no longer a victim, because you have seen Joseph in the pit, David in the cave, and Jesus on the cross all rise with the same refusal to let pain have the final word.

You have built mental toughness the way athletes build muscle: rep by rep, hard thought by hard thought, choosing to stay present with God when every part of you wanted to quit. You now know that endurance is not the absence of pain but the presence of purpose.

You can regulate your emotions in the heat of the moment because you have lengthened the sacred gap between trigger and reaction. You have learned to breathe, to name what you feel, to hand it to Jesus before you hand it to everyone else.

You regulate daily thinking the way you once regulated nothing. Morning broadcasts, evening downloads, Scripture-soaked neural pathways; these are now your non-negotiables, because you finally understand that consistency compounds and small obediences create massive freedom.

You live vision-driven, thinking from the future God promised instead of toward the past you survived. You have written the vision, made it plain, and you read it aloud every morning until the person you are becoming starts showing up in the person you are today.

You feed and fuel your brain like the temple it is. Water, omega-3s, sleep, whole foods; these are no longer optional extras but daily acts of worship that keep the three pounds of grey matter between your ears sharp enough to host the mind of Christ.

You have rewritten your inner narrative. The old tapes are shredded. The horror film is over. You now hear "beloved," "chosen," "redeemed," "more than a conqueror" when you talk to yourself, because you have let God's voice become louder than every other voice that ever tried to define you.

And now you are living as your highest self; not an improved, upgraded, hustling version of you, but Christ fully formed in you, the hope of glory. You wake up with God, move your body with gratitude, eat with reverence, say no with confidence, forgive quickly, love fiercely, and rest without guilt, because you finally believe that the abundant life is not a reward for the perfect; it is the inheritance of the surrendered.

You are not the same.

The panic attacks that once owned your nights have lost their address. The depression that used to greet you every morning has been served an eviction notice. The rage that leaked onto your children has been replaced by patience you didn't know you possessed. The marriage that was barely breathing is now laughing again. The calling that felt buried under shame is rising from the grave.

You did not just read a book. You waged war and won territory the enemy thought he would hold forever.

This is only the beginning.

Keep championing your thoughts. Keep mastering your emotions. Keep living as the highest self Jesus died to release in you.

Because the same power that raised Christ from the dead is still at work in you, demolishing strongholds, renewing your mind, and leading you into freedom you have only tasted so far.

You are not a survivor. You are a conqueror. And conquerors don't just make it through the battle; they advance the Kingdom with every healed wound and every renewed mind.

So go. Think victorious thoughts. Feel surrendered emotions. Live the highest life.

The world is waiting for the version of you that only freedom could produce.

And freedom looks unstoppable on you.

In the love of Jesus and the power of His Spirit, keep going.

The best is not behind you. The best is in you. Now let it out.

You have everything you need. Now live like it.

Romans 8:37 *"No, in all these things we are more than conquerors through him who loved us."*

REFERENCES

Adams, K., Lee, H., Patel, R., Kim, J., Thompson, E., & Nguyen, T. (2021). Chronic inflammation and cognitive decline: The role of diet-induced systemic inflammation. *Journal of Neuroinflammation, 18*(1), Article 112. https://doi.org/10.1186/s12974-021-02145-8

Ames, B. N., Grant, K. J., & Park, Y. (2021). Vitamin E and cognitive health: Mechanisms and epidemiological evidence. *Antioxidants, 10*(8), Article 1258. https://doi.org/10.3390/antiox10081258

Begum, N., & Richardson, M. (2020). B-vitamin deficiency and cognitive impairment in older adults: A systematic review. *Nutritional Neuroscience, 23*(11), 857–869. https://doi.org/10.1080/1028415X.2019.1575987

Davis, S., Peterson, L., Andrews, R., & Miller, K. (2018). Choline intake and cognitive performance: Evidence from population-based studies. *American Journal of Clinical Nutrition, 108*(4), 798–806. https://doi.org/10.1093/ajcn/nqy167

Ford, J. D. (2017). Emotion regulation and skills-based interventions. In S. N. Gold (Ed.), APA handbook of trauma psychology: Trauma practice (pp. 227–252). American Psychological Association. https://doi.org/10.1037/0000020-011

Guerrera, M. P., Volpe, S. L., & Mao, J. J. (2018). Therapeutic uses of magnesium in neurological disorders: A review. *Nutrients, 10*(7), Article 918. https://doi.org/10.3390/nu10070918

Harrison, F. E., Bowman, G. L., & May, J. M. (2022). Vitamin C function in the brain: Vital role in neuroprotection and cognitive performance. *Free Radical Biology and Medicine, 182*, 147–163. https://doi.org/10.1016/j.freeradbiomed.2022.02.013

Jernerén, F., Elshorbagy, A. K., Oulhaj, A., Smith, S. M., Refsum, H., & Smith, A. D. (2020). Brain atrophy in cognitively impaired elderly: The importance of long-chain ω-3 fatty acids and B vitamin status in a randomized controlled trial. *American Journal of Clinical Nutrition, 102*(1), 215–221. https://doi.org/10.3945/ajcn.114.103283

Johnson, R., Bryant, S., Huntley, A. L., & SWIFT Study Group. (2019). The Mediterranean diet, cognitive function, and dementia: A systematic review of the evidence. *Ageing Research Reviews, 55*, Article 100936. https://doi.org/10.1016/j.arr.2019.100936

Jones, B., Müller, C., & Schmidt, T. (2020). Dietary antioxidants and neurodegenerative diseases: A review of clinical trials. *Oxidative Medicine and Cellular Longevity, 2020*, Article 8972084. https://doi.org/10.1155/2020/8972084

Norvilitis, J. M., & Mao, Y. (2013). Attitudes toward money and credit card usage in college students: The role of need for cognition and locus of control. Journal of Applied Social Psychology, 43(1), 71–79. https://doi.org/10.1111/jasp.12001

Rahman, A., Khan, K. M., Al-Khureyzi, M., & Al-Musharaf, S. (2021). Zinc and cognitive function: A systematic review. *Nutrients, 13*(8), Article 2739. https://doi.org/10.3390/nu13082739

Smith, J., & Johnson, A. (2022). Nutrition and brain health: A life-course approach. *Annual Review of Nutrition, 42*, 287–310. https://doi.org/10.1146/annurev-nutr-062320-114628

Smith, J., Johnson, A., Lee, M., & Patel, R. (2021). Micronutrients and cognitive performance across the lifespan. *Advances in Nutrition, 12*(4), 1456–1472. https://doi.org/10.1093/advances/nmaa177

Williams, M., Woollett, K., & Criado-Perez, C. (2023). The gut-brain axis: Emerging evidence on microbiome modulation of mood and cognition. *Nature Reviews Gastroenterology & Hepatology, 20*(3), 165–182. https://doi.org/10.1038/s41575-022-00712-4

www.ingramcontent.com/pod-product-compliance
Lightning Source LLC
Chambersburg PA
CBHW071759120626
46550CB00002B/850